THE ILLINOIS CHRONICLES

THE STORY OF THE STATE OF ILLINOIS FROM ITS BIRTH TO THE PRESENT DAY

Written by Mark Skipworth. Created by Christopher Lloyd. Editorial research by Julie Deegan. Production by Nick Saul and Ali Glossop. Picture research by Felicity Page. Editorial contributions: Samuel Wheeler, James Cornelius, Peter Harbison, Christian McWhirter, Bob Cavanagh, Chris Wills, Karen Corken, Mary Reynolds, Katie Elvidge, Stuart Layne. Design by Grade Design. With special thanks to Andy Plattner. Published by What on Earth Publishing (North America) Ltd in association with Illinois200. First published in the USA in 2018 by What on Earth Publishing (North America). Copyright © 2018. All rights reserved.

ISBN: 978-0-9955770-1-5
BISAC: JNF025180 Juvenile Nonfiction / History / United States / State & Local / Illinois
JNF038190 Juvenile Nonfiction / People & Places / United States / General / US Midwest

Sears: Illinois—History—Chronology
Illinois—History—Miscellanea

LC: Illinois—Juvenile literature
Illinois—Chronology—History—Juvenile literature

whatonearthbooks.com
illinois200.com

THE ILLINOIS CHRONICLES

DANIEL POPE COOK

JAMES MONROE

BIRTH OF THE 21ST STATE

PRESIDENT MONROE SIGNS ACT ADMITTING ILLINOIS TO UNION

By our politics correspondent
December 4, 1818

THE PEOPLE of Illinois awoke today to find themselves citizens of the 21st State of the Union following a night of parties to celebrate the Territory's rise to statehood.

The historic act signed by President James Monroe is the culmination of months of hard work preparing for the big day. It is also thanks to the efforts of tireless campaigners like Mr. Daniel Pope Cook who have criticized "undemocratic" territorial government.

The new state is equally grateful to Mr. Cook's uncle, Nathaniel Pope, who helped draft the bill that went to the United States Congress. The Illinois border has been moved 51 miles farther north so that the State benefits from its own shoreline along Lake Michigan, giving access to the Great Lakes.

A constitutional convention of 33 delegates was held last July in Kaskaskia, the new State capital. Some believe Illinois does not have the 40,000 citizens required for statehood. But, perhaps by counting some people twice and those passing through, the number has been reached.

The Constitution—framed in large part by the brilliant young Randolph County delegate, Mr. Elias Kent Kane—has been approved by Congress, and the new General Assembly is now able to pass laws.

Mr. Shadrach Bond, the first delegate to Congress from the Illinois Territory, has been chosen as first governor, the new head of state.

Only time will tell whether the Constitution's anti-slavery principle holds. Farmers, particularly those close to the western frontier, previously voiced concerns about competition from others using enslaved labor.

President Monroe had earlier expressed a poor opinion of our great land, reportedly describing it as "miserably poor" with grasslands that "will not have a bush on them for ages." He was wrong: the "Prairie State" has come a long way since the French used the name of local Native Americans to identify it. Bordered by two great rivers, the Mississippi and Ohio, Illinois connects the southern and eastern states, and is blessed with natural resources including the lead ore of Galena.

The trading post that stands beside Fort Dearborn on the Chicago River, with access to both the Great Lakes and the Mississippi, is certain to go from strength to strength.

Pioneers are also finding uncultivated prairie soils can produce healthy crops. Families from the tobacco-growing South are making a new start in the wooded hills of southern Illinois, leading some to call it the "Sucker State" in a possible uncharitable reference to the "suckers" that sprout off tobacco plants and take away nutrients.

Statehood will be costly after the United States government stops paying for public officials in Illinois, but Mr. Cook insists a new wave of settlers will increase land values.

The star of Illinois will be added to the Union flag from next year, as is the custom for new admissions, on Independence Day, July 4.

FROM TOWN TO CITY IN JUST 4 YEARS

By our politics editor
March 5, 1837

THE TOWN of Chicago became a city yesterday in an official proclamation ceremony to change its legal status. This will be remembered as the day Chicago claimed its place as one of the most important centers in the Midwest. It has been a remarkable rise, from a town of a few hundred residents to a city of about 4,000 in only four years.

Not so long ago it was just the Fort Dearborn trading post, whose first settler was reputed to be Mr. Jean Baptiste Point DuSable of French and African Haitian descent. Land beside the Chicago River was later obtained from the Potawatomi Native American people, and the settlement grew.

Now, thanks to the Chicago Portage, the city is an expanding transportation hub, with its own lighthouse to direct traffic from Lake Michigan. With the removal of Native Americans, Fort Dearborn, sited beside the river, has outlived its use.

Few Chicagoans will forget the ceremony some years ago when hundreds of Native Americans wearing traditional body paint and eagle and hawk feathers gathered in the town for a cermonial dance, possibly for the last time in Illinois, just before their departure for lands west of the Mississippi.

But the city will always be indebted to the Native Americans for its name, which some say means "wild onions" or "garlic" that once grew profusely on nearby marshes.

Mob Claims Life of Anti-Slavery Campaigner

OUTSPOKEN JOURNALIST and Presbyterian minister, Elijah Parish Lovejoy was murdered yesterday by a mob as his new printing press was delivered to a warehouse in Alton, *writes our crime correspondent, November 8, 1837.*

Mr. Lovejoy was known for his editorials and sermons against those using or allowing enslaved labor. He moved to "anti-slavery" Illinois after having printing presses destroyed in St. Louis. However, in Alton he was told to leave by residents but defiantly insisted freedom of speech is protected by the U.S. Constitution.

Witnesses say the printing press had been delivered when violence broke out. Shots were fired and several lay dead, including Mr. Lovejoy. He was aged 34.

Leading abolitionists are calling him a martyr. John Brown said Mr. Lovejoy's death had led him to vow to "consecrate my life to the destruction of slavery."

ILLINOIS' OWN TRAIL OF TEARS

By our news correspondent
March 31, 1839

STORIES ARE circulating that an unimaginable and surely avoidable tragedy has occurred in southern Illinois with the deaths of hundreds of Native Americans while being forcibly relocated to distant designated lands west of the Mississippi.

Thousands of Cherokee men, women, and children have been marching on a 1,000-mile trek to a new "Indian Territory" after gold was discovered in Georgia, their traditional homeland. It is understood they were forced to leave to make way for European settlers planning to exploit the vacated farmland.

The deaths are being attributed to a combination of the sheer distance to be traveled through the harsh Midwest winter, aggravated by clothing inadequate for the weather, along with the absence of food supplies and even footwear —many marching for hundreds of miles barefoot through the mud, ice, and snow.

The first group of marchers crossed into southern Illinois in December. A U.S. agent who helped to oversee their removal, wrote: "There is the coldest weather in Illinois I ever experienced anywhere. The streams are all frozen over...We are compelled to cut through the ice to get water for ourselves... There is no possible chance of crossing the (Mississippi) river for the numerous quantity of ice that comes floating down."

According to observers, it has taken nearly three months for the Cherokee families, many of them starving, to cross the 60 miles of land between the Ohio and Mississippi rivers. Some estimate up to 4,000–6,000 of those who set out on the trek may have died in the bitter conditions.

Native Americans are said to refer to these forced marches as "The Trail of Tears."

NEW HARVESTER BOOSTS FARMING

INGENIOUS HORSE-DRAWN REAPER CUTS, THRESHES, AND BALES ALL IN ONE GO

By our agriculture correspondent
May 2, 1851

MR. CYRUS McCormick's amazing new mechanical reaper has proved an international sensation at the Great Exhibition of the Works of Industry of All Nations in London, England.

Chicago-based Mr. McCormick traveled to England himself to display his harvesting machine at the Crystal Palace, and was yesterday awarded a medal for his invention. Among the dignitaries supporting the exhibition are Queen Victoria and Prince Albert, Charles Darwin, Charlotte Brontë, and Charles Dickens. Mr. McCormick's prize follows the success of Mr. John Deere, of Moline, whose moldboard plow has allowed far more land of the Midwest prairies to be cultivated.

Friends of Mr. McCormick say it was the proudest day of his life, recognition for all the years spent overcoming problems with his invention's reliability to help revolutionize agriculture. They also say he would be the first to acknowledge the debt he owes his father Robert, also an inventor, who spent 20 years developing a mechanical reaper, though it never proved reliable enough.

Virginia-born Mr. McCormick took out his first patent in 1834 for a horse-drawn machine that would automatically cut, thresh, and bundle grain. He showed how, with little effort, it could increase farms' yield tenfold. He recalled with amusement that farmers were skeptical of the reaper at first, with some of them unkind enough to describe it as moving like an elephant, and insisting that men could harvest the grain just as fast without it.

He admitted his invention only started to catch on after many workers in the Midwest left for the new territories further west and the California gold rush, creating labor shortages. Taking advantage of Chicago as a transportation hub, he has established a factory in the city to sell his machines across North America.

Devoutly religious, Mr. McCormick says he believes it is his mission to feed the world.

Religious Minority Forced To Flee Their Homes In Nauvoo

MORMONS STARTED a modern-day exodus from the town of Nauvoo yesterday following the death of founder Mr. Joseph Smith, killed two years ago by a mob, *writes our religion correspondent, February 5, 1846.*

They are thought to be heading west for the Salt Lake Valley in Utah after intimidation from non-Mormon residents in surrounding Hancock County. Mr. Brigham Young is understood to be the main organizer.

Some residents said they felt ashamed that the Mormons were being forced to leave their homes at the hands of local folk.

Others in the county, however, said the town had become a state within a state, the Mormons having their own government and even their own legal militia. They also accused some followers of having more than one wife.

Mr. Smith brought the Mormons, followers of the Church of Christ of Latter-day Saints, from Missouri to escape conflict there. They purchased woodland around the town of Commerce, renamed by Mr. Smith "Nauvoo" from the Hebrew for "beautiful place." Under the Mormons, the town has flourished. With 12,000 inhabitants, it rivals the growing city of Chicago.

Accused of ordering the destruction of a critical newspaper's printing press, Mr. Smith was awaiting trial in jail for inciting a riot, later increased to the charge of treason. A mob stormed the jail, fatally wounding Mr. Smith and his brother Hyrum.

After the killings the "Nauvoo charter" was repealed, leaving the community without adequate government or militia.

Mr. Smith, who introduced baptism for the dead, is seen by Mormons as a prophet and martyr to his faith.

By our politics editor
June 17, 1858

"A HOUSE DIVIDED AGAINST ITSELF CANNOT STAND"

SPRINGFIELD LAWYER Mr. Abraham Lincoln, a Republican nominee for the U.S. Senate, yesterday delivered the speech of a great statesman that will resound across America as a warning of the threat to the Union over the slavery debate.

Using words from the Bible, Mr. Lincoln made clear his opposition to expanding slavery into new U.S. territories and spoke of a looming crisis that would pass only after it has been resolved once and for all.

"A house divided against itself cannot stand. I believe this government cannot endure, permanently half slave and half free," he said. "I do not expect the Union to be dissolved—I do not expect the house to fall—but I do expect it will cease to be divided. It will become all one thing, or all the other."

He added: "Either the opponents of slavery will arrest the further spread of it, and place it where the public mind shall rest in the belief that it is in course of ultimate extinction; or its advocates will push it forward, till it shall become alike lawful in all the States, old as well as new—North as well as South."

Mr. Lincoln was, in effect, laying down a challenge to the nation: that we, its citizens, must now decide which route we are to go down. His speech, made in the Illinois State Capitol in Springfield, has been acclaimed by abolitionists and Republican supporters. Some were saying last night that Mr. Lincoln has shown he has the qualities needed to become a great U.S. President.

Reaction in the southern "Slave States" is unlikely to be positive. Some are already warning of seceding from the Union and the risk of civil war if men like Mr. Lincoln ever get to hold national office. Mr. Lincoln is due to embark on a series of debates across Illinois with U.S. Senator Stephen Douglas, the Democratic incumbent. The slavery issue is certain to be high on the agenda.

A German version of Mr. Lincoln's speech is also to be printed in Alton for the State's German-speaking residents.

> Illinois is a major source of troops for the Union with 250,000 serving in the Civil War. It is also an important provider of military supplies. Galena's Ulysses S. Grant is made U.S. Army commander, and forces the Confederate commander Robert E. Lee to surrender at Appomattox. Grant is twice elected U.S. President.

Mr. Lincoln's New Whiskers

PRESIDENT-ELECT Lincoln yesterday stopped on his inaugural journey by train from Illinois to Washington, D.C. and met an old friend —a 12-year-old girl, *writes our politics correspondent, February 17, 1861.*

The meeting between Mr. Lincoln and Miss Grace Bedell took place in her hometown of Westfield, New York. Onlookers were surprised to hear him look for the little girl and ask for her by name.

Miss Bedell had written to Mr. Lincoln last year urging him to grow a beard. Her letter read: "I hope you won't think me very bold to write to such a great man as you are...If you let your whiskers grow...you would look a great deal better for your face is so thin." Mr. Lincoln wrote back that never having worn any whiskers, people might think it a "silly affectation" to start now. He signed it "Your very sincere well wisher." Despite his doubts, he took the advice, and grew a beard while in Springfield. At yesterday's meeting, Mr. Lincoln stooped down and kissing Miss Bedell, said: "Gracie, look at my whiskers. I have been growing them for you!"

Mr. Lincoln is also an inventor, having a patent granted, for re-floating boats in shallow waters using his "Improved Method of Lifting Vessels over Shoals."

TOMB RAIDERS FOILED

By our crime correspondent
November 8, 1876

A FIENDISH PLOT to steal the late President Lincoln's body and ransom it for $200,000 was foiled by detectives yesterday.

Members of an Illinois gang are on the run after failing to make off with the remains of the President who was assassinated in Washington, D.C., over a decade ago. The gang traveled to Oak Ridge Cemetery in Springfield, where the President's body is laid to rest and is now considered a shrine to liberty.

They sawed a padlock off the iron door of his tomb, pried the marble lid off his sarcophagus, and attempted to lift the coffin. The theft was thwarted when Lewis G. Swegles, an undercover secret service agent who had been unwittingly recruited by the gang, alerted detectives hiding nearby. They rushed to the tomb, guns drawn, but the robbers escaped.

Gang leader "Big Jim" Kinealy is said to have hatched the plot to steal the President's body until $200,000 in gold was paid by the U.S. government and an imprisoned gang member freed.

Sources said last night it was not the first time Kinealy had planned such a raid. The previous attempt did not get off the ground after drunken gang members revealed details of the plot in Springfield.

The latest incident is certain to increase calls for the President's body to be buried rather than kept in a sarcophagus.

INFERNO LEAVES CHICAGO IN RUINS

HUNDREDS KILLED—MANY HOMES, CHURCHES, AND BUSINESSES DESTROYED

By our city correspondent
October 11, 1871

CHICAGOANS TODAY surveyed the ruins of their once great city—and wept. In just over 30 hours, the Great Fire has destroyed 17,500 buildings, killed up to 300 people and left a third of its 300,000 residents homeless as winter approaches.

Investigators are seeking to establish the cause of the blaze, but it is thought to have started in or close to a barn belonging to Mr. Patrick O'Leary on DeKoven Street. It is rumored a cow owned by his wife, Mrs. Catherine O'Leary, accidentally knocked over a lantern setting fire to straw.

Civic leaders admit the fire could have been contained had the city used materials other than wood for many of its buildings. Even the sidewalks were wooden. A drought had made the buildings tinder-dry while strong southwest winds whipped up flames to a conflagration.

Witnesses describe how "waves of fire" engulfed offices, hotels, churches, stores, and factories. One says the blaze devoured buildings as if they had been the "playthings of a child." Others report that many were trapped in the downtown area, and fled to the beaches along Lake Michigan. Some resorted to burying themselves in the sand to avoid the flames. Fire ran up the rigging of boats turning masts into giant candles before consuming the hulls.

It is no surprise the city's Fire Department was overwhelmed. The courageous efforts of its firefighters were not enough to overcome the tornado-like "fire whirls" that spread flaming debris far and wide.

The blaze began to die down only after rains arrived late on Monday night, leaving a huge area of devastation. An appeal has now gone out across America and overseas to provide assistance to those most in need of help.

U.S. President Ulysses S. Grant, who made his home in northern Illinois before moving to the White House, is understood to be donating $1,000 of his own money.

Despite the devastation, civic leaders predict the city will rise rapidly from the ashes. It is said fortunes are there to be made by those willing to invest in the new Chicago.

Almost all prominent buildings have been destroyed, the Chicago Water Tower being one of a handful to survive, and is certain to be cherished as a reminder to future generations. Ironically, O'Leary's own cottage was left standing after the blaze.

One Two Three— Up She Goes!

THE RAISING of a Chicago landmark six feet in the air has been successfully completed to make way for the city's new sewage system, thanks to an ingenious feat of engineering, *writes our technology correspondent, March 15, 1861.*

The Tremont House hotel, from the balcony of which both Abraham Lincoln and Stephen Douglas gave speeches, stayed open throughout the operation that lasted several weeks. It is said some guests did not even notice anything was happening.

To hoist the hotel, 5,000 jackscrews were placed beneath the building's foundations. One man was assigned to operate each section of 10 jackscrews. On the signal, each man turned the jackscrews the same amount at the same time, and the six-story building slowly lifted. It is one of many buildings, including the one pictured below, raised to the new street level for sewers to be installed beneath.

The engineering feat follows protests from Chicagoans about the city's poor sanitation after a cholera outbreak seven years ago. Because it stands just above Lake Michigan's shores, the city has little or no natural drainage and thus harbors disease. It has gained the unenviable and accurate nickname "Mud Hole of the Prairies."

City planners decided on an underground sewage system but the low-level ground meant lowering the Chicago River or raising the city. They chose the latter.

The waste water is already draining more efficiently but some engineers predict it will not be long before the Chicago River becomes an open sewer, threatening to pollute drinking water and be a general risk to health.

SATISFACTION GUARANTEED—BY MAIL ORDER

By our business editor
January 31, 1875

OWNERS OF small-town stores in the Midwest reacted furiously yesterday to a mail-order catalog from Montgomery Ward, some even burning copies of it in public.

They claim its 100-plus pages of "dry goods...at the lowest wholesale prices" could destroy their trade with rural customers by offering them a wider choice at bargain prices than they could ever match. Montgomery Ward —whose advertising slogan is "Satisfaction guaranteed or your money back"—is certain to become a firm favorite in rural Midwest homes, its free catalog selling everything from sewing machines to barbed wire.

Company founder Mr. Aaron Montgomery Ward, supported by his brother-in-law Mr. George Thorne, has been hailed a pioneer in mail order. As a traveling salesman, he had witnessed the poor value for money Midwest settlers often received from small-town stores when buying general merchandise. He decided to make full use of the expanding railroad network centered on Chicago.

> The invention of barbed wire was developed and popularized by Illinois-based businessmen including John Glidden and Isaac Ellwood in DeKalb. Chicago-born John Warne Gates was a promoter of barbed wire in Texas, and became a steel magnate.

TOWERING OFFICES RISE FROM ASHES OF OLD CHICAGO

By our city editor
August 24, 1885

A 10-STORY building in Chicago is poised to become the world's first "skyscraper," and change the skyline of one of America's greatest cities for ever. Rising to an amazing height of 138 feet, the Home Insurance Building has an innovative structure that uses a metal skeleton frame from which are hung "curtain walls" of stone and brick.

Thus, the building weighs much less than if built using more traditional construction techniques. These would have required thicker walls at the base to support the weight of the building above.

The innovative design will allow buildings to be taller and slimmer than their predecessors, with more internal space and greater window areas for natural light.

The rebuilding of the new Chicago is now in full swing after the Great Fire destroyed almost all of the downtown area.

One journalist has observed that construction on such a scale is "a miracle of pleasing sensations and fascinating scenes" that makes him feel "ecstatic."

The Home Insurance Building is the work of Mr. William LeBaron Jenney who won a competition for plans for the site, resistance to fire being a key consideration in awarding the contract.

Mr. Jenney was educated in engineering and architecture at the prestigious École Centrale Paris, graduating a year after his fellow student M. Gustave Eiffel, who is planning a gigantic metal tower in the French capital. During the Civil War, Mr. Jenney designed numerous fortifications for the Union side.

The iron-and-steel skeleton of the Home Insurance Building is claimed to offer greater protection against fire, which will reassure workers in a city that is still recovering from the tragic inferno that devastated the downtown area in 1871.

MAGNET FOR SOCIAL REFORM
ILLINOIS ACTIVIST PIONEERS A BETTER LIFE FOR ALL

By our communities editor
September 18, 1890

A SHINING LIGHT in the settlement movement, Hull-House in Chicago's West Side today celebrates its first year of operation.

The growing complex of buildings in one of the city's poorest neighborhoods is the brainchild of Miss Jane Addams and co-founder Miss Ellen Gates Starr. They have sought to provide a refuge from poverty for scores of newly arrived immigrants.

Their radical approach has grabbed the nation's attention after establishing America's first settlement house as a place where better-off members of society can live among the poor to improve their lives through education, culture, and learning.

Miss Addams, born into a prosperous Cedarville family and whose father is an Illinois State legislator, has chosen to live at Hull-House in order to make practical improvements to her new neighborhood.

Italians, Germans, Greeks, and Jews are among those living in filthy conditions on the West Side, often without a water supply or connection to a street sewer. They have flocked to Hull-House after Miss Addams paid for repairs to the rundown mansion to create a night school for adults, kindergarten, clubs for children, a gym, bathhouse, music school, and library. In addition to teaching about nutrition and health, there is help from visitors, including a "community of university women," for people to learn new skills to find better jobs.

Inspired by Toynbee Hall in England, the world's first settlement house, Miss Addams believes passionately in feeding the soul as well as the body, with reading groups and lectures on art and music.

This "mother to the nation" is also making waves in the field of social research. Live-in female residents are helping to develop Hull-House as a research center, undertaking studies on living conditions in the neighborhood and on child labor.

As Hull-House becomes a magnet for social reform to improve people's lives, many see Miss Addams as a modern-day saint.

Union Stock Yard is hog butcher and meatpacker for the world

AS MANY AS 12 million cattle and hogs passed through Chicago's Union Stock Yard in the last 12 months, according to an end-of-year estimate, *writes our commerce correspondent, December 31, 1890.*

The figure represents a four-fold increase in 20 years and means that the yard is now the butcher for the nation and beyond. Already a major railroad hub, the Windy City was

an obvious choice to locate a meat-processing industry when demand soared to feed Union troops fighting in the Civil War.

The yard came into being back in 1865 after a group of railroad companies acquired swampland in southwest Chicago and built 15 miles of track to connect the meatpacking district to the main lines. With over 2,000 separate

livestock pens for cattle, hogs, and sheep, the yard has overtaken industry rivals in Cincinnati.

Thousands of men are now employed in meatpacking plants across a vast area. Health officials, however, are increasingly concerned about threats to the city's drinking water as so much stockyard waste is draining into the Chicago River. Its south fork has

been nicknamed "Bubbly Creek" because of the gases produced from decomposition.

The authorities are becoming worried about the growing settlement of German, Irish, and Czech migrants that has come to be known as "Back of the Yards" where, they say, squalor and poverty are sure to lead to outbreaks of disease.

A MODERN WONDER OF THE WORLD

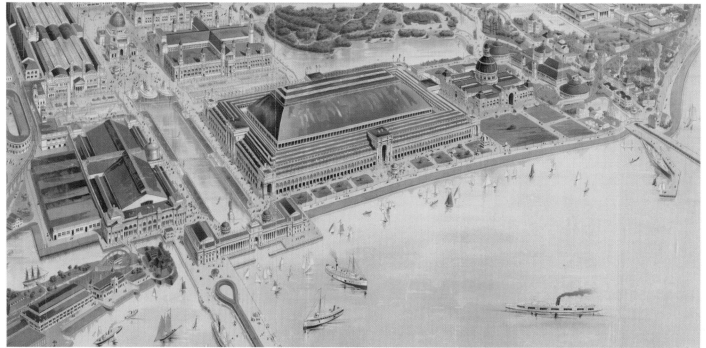

By our city editor
May 2, 1893

CHICAGO CAME of age as a great international city yesterday when the World's Fair opened to delighted crowds with magic, razzamatazz, and stunning innovations that preview the next century.

The first World's Columbian Exposition, held to celebrate the 400th anniversary of Christopher Columbus' arrival in the New World, was instantly acclaimed a "modern wonder of the age" with around 200 buildings dedicated to displays from every corner of the globe.

Under the supervision of works director Mr. Daniel Burnham, the temporary structures have been covered in plaster and painted white to gleam in the sun. This "White City" is illuminated at night to breathtaking effect by hundreds of electric lights.

There has been nothing like it seen in America. Visitors were visibly awestruck yesterday.

After the U.S. Congress authorized a world's fair, Chicago beat a campaign by New York City to stage it. Yesterday, the fairgrounds, sited on a converted two-mile swamp on the shores of Lake Michigan, were officially opened by President Cleveland.

Their scale must be seen to be believed. Most states and 46 nations have exhibits. California's features a knight on horseback made entirely of prunes.

There are snake-charmers, Venetian gondolas, German artillery, and even a replica Viking ship. A belly-dancer beguiled crowds yesterday in the Streets of Cairo exhibit. At least 3,000 drinking fountains have also been

installed around the grounds. In Midway Plaisance stands an imaginative "Eskimaux Village," while Mrs. Bertha Palmer's Woman's Building is located nearby.

It is the technical innovations which stole the show yesterday, among them the first steam turbine and an electric train. Visitors also got a taste for the new snack food called "popcorn."

Star attraction is the giant wheel, an engineering marvel and world-first, built by Mr. George W. Ferris. Immediately labeled the "Ferris wheel," it surely rivals the Paris exposition's Eiffel Tower.

The 264-feet-high wheel carries 36 cars, each holding up to 60 people. Its axle alone weighs 70 tons and thus ensures the wheel is strong enough to lift as many as 2,000 people at a time high above the fairgrounds.

The fair is not without its controversy. Miss Ida B. Wells, the civil rights campaigner, has arrived in Chicago to protest the exclusion of exhibits from African Americans unless approved by all-white committees. Department store owner Mr. Marshall Field has pledged he is ready to donate funds for a museum to house some of the wonderful artifacts that will be left behind when the fair closes in October.

Death of a Monster

CRAZED SERIAL killer H. H. Holmes was hanged yesterday for the murder of a longtime colleague, but investigators believe his horrendous crimes may have resulted in the deaths of dozens more victims, *writes our crime correspondent, May 8, 1896.*

The former medical graduate moved to Chicago, and opened a hotel in Englewood in which he built a labyrinth of rooms and stairways, some leading to nowhere.

The hotel has come to be known as "Murder Castle" after it emerged that he had been doing away with his mainly female staff and guests, often selling their body parts to medical schools to conceal the evidence.

"I was born with the devil in me," he once said.

ENGINEERING MARVEL DEFIES NATURE

THE WATERS of the Chicago River are today flowing AWAY from Lake Michigan – and that's the way they are going to remain, *writes our engineering correspondent, January 3, 1900.*

In one of the largest earth-moving operations ever undertaken in America, the river now empties into the new Chicago Sanitary and Ship Canal with a series of giant locks used to increase the flow from Lake Michigan.

In a remarkable feat of engineering, this has permanently reversed the flow in an effort to end the threat of water-borne diseases from drains and sewers. City leaders took the momentous decision after previous projects

failed to fully tackle the filthy state of the river. As Chicago booms, sewage and factory waste continues to blight the river while polluted drinking water is still claiming lives.

A series of water intake "cribs" for Chicago's water supplies were built in Lake Michigan far away from its polluted shoreline, and brought some improvement, as did the closure of all shoreline sewage outlets around the time of the World's Columbian Exposition.

The river was first reversed nearly 30 years ago but the flow could revert to its natural direction when overwhelmed by storms. Heavy rains 15 years ago washed refuse out into the lake, raising fears that

sewage might one day reach the water intakes, and cause a disease epidemic.

City leaders say the 28-mile canal, which connects to the Des Plaines River, guarantees that even in the worst weather, the river can now always flow away from the lake. The new canal is deeper and wider than the old Illinois and Michigan Canal, allowing larger ships to navigate between the Great Lakes and the Mississippi River, a further boost for trade across the continent.

But this engineering triumph has not been met with universal approval. The State of Missouri is threatening to bring a court action against Illinois to stop any sewage getting into the Mississippi River.

A MASTERPIECE OF ARCHITECTURE

By our arts correspondent
December 30, 1904

A SPRINGFIELD MANSION built for a wealthy heiress and socialite is being hailed as a showcase for the genius of Chicago-based Mr. Frank Lloyd Wright and his "Prairie" style of architecture.

Experts say that the 35-roomed Illinois building is Mr. Wright's masterpiece. Inspired by Midwest landscapes, it features such "signature" touches as low-angled roofs and

art-glass windows displaying chevrons that evoke prairie sumac trees, along with bold lines and geometric shapes.

The interior has open spaces more suitable for modern American lifestyles than traditional grand houses, and includes large interconnecting reception areas for entertainment—it even has galleries for musicians to play to guests below.

The house took two years to build after it was commissioned by Mrs. Susan Lawrence Dana, a widow, who has now staged a festive

party to show off her magnificent new home to the elite of Illinois society.

Mr. Wright, the rising star of a new movement in architecture, was asked to remodel her family's home but the design and rebuild went far beyond that, and have effectively created an entirely new house.

One expert predicted Mr. Wright's American style will make him internationally famous, and that house builders up and down the country and around the world will come to adopt many of his novel design features.

ILLINOIS WOMEN WIN THE VOTE

By our politics editor
June 27, 1913

THE Illinois General Assembly yesterday granted women the right to vote for U.S. President, the first state east of the Mississippi to do so.

The passing of the Municipal Voting Act, which also allows women to vote for some local officials, has been acclaimed as a landmark in the national suffrage movement.

At least 250,000 women are expected to vote in forthcoming Illinois elections. Campaigners hailed the victory as a great day for democracy—and a great day for women.

Much of the credit must go to Mrs. Grace Wilbur Trout and her supporters who organized a brilliant lobbying campaign.

The Bill passed the Illinois Senate first, and was brought up for a House of Representatives vote about a fortnight ago.

Mrs. Trout, recently elected president of the Illinois Equal Suffrage Association, arranged visits to the homes of absent pro-suffrage Representatives to bring them out to vote. She also organized the first Suffrage Automobile Tour of Illinois, and was seen guarding the door to the House chambers

and urging members in favor of the Bill not to leave without voting. The Bill passed 83 to 58, and was yesterday signed into law by Governor Dunne.

Association members overcame stiff opposition from many men. One wrote that women had done nothing to deserve the vote and that they

were merely the "hostile instruments by which humanity is created."

A debt of thanks is also owed to early campaigners, pictured above, including Miss Frances Willard, leader of the Woman's Christian Temperance Union. She battled in Springfield for the right of women to vote on the sale of liquor.

The new law is only a partial victory: women can vote for President but not for Governor or Congressman, and have to use separate ballot boxes from men.

Men who are African American or naturalized immigrants have been given full voting rights, so the fight goes on across America.

America Takes Jungle Hero To Its Heart

Edgar Rice Burroughs

THE IMAGINATION of America and the world has been captured by *Tarzan of the Apes*, the sell-out novel and cultural sensation created by Chicago-born author Mr. Edgar Rice Burroughs, *writes our books editor, June 30, 1914.*

First published in a magazine two years ago, the book tells the story of Tarzan, born John Clayton, the son of a British lord and lady who are marooned on the west coast of Africa by mutineers. When John is just a year old, his mother dies of natural

causes and his father is killed by the leader of a troop of great apes.

The orphan is rescued by Kala, a kindly female ape who adopts and raises the boy as her own. He grows up to be known as Tarzan and has many adventures in Africa.

Mr. Burroughs, of Oak Park, tried his hand at pulp fiction after less-than-successful careers as a soldier and cowboy. But all this will be forgotten with the runaway success of the jungle hero he has created, and the fortune it will make for him.

He now plans sequels, possible comic strips, and merchandise. There is even talk of turning Tarzan into a movie. The paying public, it seems, just can't get enough of Mr. Burroughs' jungle hero.

Commentators say his mixture of adventure and romance will inspire boys and girls for generations to come. The story is bound to capture the attention of the Chicago film industry, which already boasts the greatest number of production companies across America.

NATIONAL DISGRACE
HUNDREDS FEARED DEAD IN VIOLENT RACE RIOTS

By our civil rights correspondent
July 3, 1917

EAST ST. LOUIS, the industrial city on the eastern shores of the Mississippi, is today counting the appalling cost of some of the worst race riots ever seen in America. Unverifiable claims suggest as many as 200 lives have been lost after white mobs went on the rampage yesterday, beating and murdering African American workers, and burning at least 250 buildings including houses, a railway warehouse, and a theater.

As the violence began to subside, Governor Lowden pledged that the National Guard would remain on the streets of the city to protect African Americans. But some have little faith in the troops who have been criticized for standing by as the violence took place.

Racial tensions have been building after workers at an aluminum plant went on strike, and African American workers were brought in their place. The strikers have yet to get their jobs back.

Such events have touched on wider fears among white workers over job security. As the U.S. economy is boosted by the Great War in Europe, East St. Louis, and other industrial centers are facing labor shortages with jobs being filled by African Americans from the South, sometimes recruited with greatly exaggerated promises of well-paid jobs.

Yesterday's violence has left hundreds of African Americans homeless. It appears entire neighborhoods have been burnt down with reports that rioters cut water hoses, preventing the Fire Department from tackling the blaze.

Jamaican politician, Mr. Marcus Garvey, condemned the rioting in East St. Louis as "one of the bloodiest outrages against mankind."

The Chamber of Commerce is furious with the mayor for allowing a "reign of lawlessness," and demands are growing for the resignation of senior police officers.

The true death toll may never be known as many of the victims have no official graves, and casual estimates vary wildly.

The riots follow race tensions in Springfield, home of Abraham Lincoln, nearly a decade ago when a white mob ran amok in an African American neighborhood.

The violence in Springfield convinced many of the need for a civil rights campaign in the U.S., leading to the founding of the National Association for the Advancement of Colored People. Its Springfield chapter was among the first to be established.

Passing of a Saint

CHICAGOANS ARE today mourning the death of their beloved Mother Cabrini, and there are calls at home and abroad for her to be made a saint, *writes our religion correspondent, December 23, 1917.*

Suffering from malaria contracted on one of her many overseas expeditions, she died yesterday, aged 67, at the Columbus Hospital she founded and named for the New World explorer.

The Italian-born missionary opened more than 70 hospitals, schools, convents, and orphanages in the U.S. and abroad, often raising funds by begging on the streets. In Chicago, her last home, she spent her final days packing candy and toys for the deprived children of "Little Italy" on the city's West Side.

Hope and peace

ILLINOIS celebrates 100 years of statehood today, heralding a new era of peace and hope for its citizens, *writes our state correspondent, December 3, 1918.*

The centennial comes less than a month after Armistice Day, which ended the fighting and horrific death toll in World War I. All told, Illinois provided more than 300,000 recruits after the U.S. entered the war.

Many Illinoisans distinguished themselves in the war, notably Lt. Col. Otis B. Duncan, from Springfield, who became the highest ranking African American officer in the American Expeditionary Forces by the end of the war.

The U.S. has emerged as a world power while Illinois goes from strength to strength. A new flag has been designed to capture this unique moment in the State's history—its first 100 years.

SAY IT AIN'T SO, JOE...

EIGHT CHICAGO White Sox baseball players accused of taking money from gamblers to deliberately lose the World Series were yesterday found not guilty by a jury, *writes our sports correspondent, August 3, 1921.*

The accused were cleared of all charges, namely that they conspired to defraud the public, commit a confidence game, and injure the business of the team's owner. In 1919, the White Sox—one of the best baseball teams ever—lost the World Series to underdogs the Cincinnati Reds. Soon after, stories began to emerge that White Sox players had received bribes to "throw" the series.

Despite yesterday's acquittals, all eight players are to be effectively expelled, and will never play major league baseball again. One story that has already gone into legend is attributed to a child, who steps up to star player "Shoeless" Joe Jackson and, grabbing his idol's coat, says: "Say it ain't so, Joe." But Jackson insists the incident simply never took place.

The "Black Sox" scandal, as it has come to be known, has rocked America's sporting world. Despite the setback, the White Sox remain an iconic team, having already won the World Series twice.

STATE HIT BY DEADLY TORNADO

IN THE TWINKLING OF AN EYE, THE TOWN OF MURPHYSBORO WAS SIMPLY NO MORE

By our weather correspondent
March 19, 1925

ILLINOISANS ARE today reeling from the deadliest tornado in U.S. history, which claimed the lives of nearly 700 people across three states and left hundreds of residents homeless.

The unprecedented Tri-State Tornado yesterday devastated towns, cities, and farms in Missouri, Illinois—where fatalities were highest—and Indiana.

It is still unclear whether the destruction was caused by a single tornado or a "tornado family" of multiple outbreaks. Either way, the ferocity of the mile-wide storm was unprecedented.

Gorham was leveled, the tornado killing or injuring about half the town's population. Murphysboro lost 234 residents and at least 150 of its 200 blocks, while 69 were killed and many homes swept away in De Soto. Nine schools across the three states were completely destroyed.

Residents said that although these are dark days for their communities, their enduring spirit and faith will ensure that their homes and livelihoods will be rebuilt.

Mother road gives birth to age of the automobile

U.S. ROUTE 66 came into being yesterday, a 2,500-mile national highway established for those migrating west by automobile and truck, *writes our transport correspondent, November 12, 1926.*

The road will run through Illinois from Chicago to Pontiac, Springfield, and East St. Louis, and on to Missouri, Kansas, Oklahoma, Texas, New Mexico, and Arizona before reaching Los Angeles in California.

Its construction follows a decision by the U.S. Congress to develop a network of national highways, though it will be at least another decade before the route is completely paved. Dedicated road signs are to be installed along the road next year, and seem set to become icons of the open road.

As the route takes shape it will boost the economy of the areas it passes through, some of them presently impoverished. So-called "mom and pop" businesses are expected to spring up along it, from filling stations to diners. Plans are afoot to build auto camps and new drive-in "motels" so that travelers can break their journeys at rest stops overnight and during the day.

The road will be the route taken by families seeking to head west as far as the Pacific. The number "66" was chosen because it was thought it would be easy to remember.

Once again, Illinois is at the center of a new national transportation network. First it was rivers and canals, then railroads, now it is the automobile.

BRAVE BESSIE DIES IN PLANE CRASH

By our aviation correspondent
May 1, 1926

BESSIE COLEMAN, America's first woman pilot of either African or Native American descent, died tragically yesterday in a flying accident. She was 34. Her daredevil stunts in Chicago helped to make her reputation as one of the world's greatest women fliers.

Miss Coleman, born in Texas with an African American mother and a father of Native and African American parentage, dropped out of college when she ran out of money.

She came to Chicago seeking a better life, and worked hard to save so that she could afford to learn how to fly.

However, as American flying schools would not admit women or African Americans, Miss Coleman took language classes and traveled to France to qualify as a pilot.

She achieved her goal at a flying school near Paris—the first pilot's license ever issued to an African American.

"Brave Bessie" will be remembered for her stunt-flying and wing-walking that amazed crowds flocked to see, as well as her daredevil aerobatics high overhead.

From the money she received from the shows, she bought three Army surplus Curtiss bi-planes which she used to open her own flying school.

But it wasn't to be. Yesterday, she took off on a test flight in Jacksonville, Florida, but went into an uncontrolled dive from which her plane never recovered. She was neither strapped in nor wearing a parachute.

Her life story is already an inspiration to African and Native Americans as well as women around the world. To her many fans, she will always be known as Bessie, the woman who "dared to dream."

MASSACRE ON ST. VALENTINE'S DAY

By our crime correspondent
February 15, 1929

THE COLD-blooded murder of seven men gunned down on Chicago's North Side yesterday morning is now believed to be the violent result of a power struggle between rival gangs for control of illegal liquor supplies in the city.

The men were shot at around 10:30 a.m. in a warehouse in the Lincoln Park neighborhood. Two of the four shooters were said to be dressed in fake police uniforms. Sub-machine guns were among the weapons used by the gangsters.

The victims are understood to include members of George "Bugs" Moran's North Side Gang. They are believed to have been lured to the garage with the promise of an illegal shipment of whiskey.

One of the victims survived the shooting but died three hours later. He was questioned by police but refused to identify the killers. He had received no less than 14 bullet wounds. However, when asked who shot him, he replied: "No one shot me."

The only survivor is a dog named Highball, owned by an associate of the Moran gang.

The massacre has all the hallmarks of gangster Al "Scarface" Capone (pictured above), increasingly seen as America's Public Enemy Number 1.

Capone, who is currently in Miami, appears to have resorted to mob violence after Moran started to muscle in on his organization's numerous criminal activities.

Police believe Moran himself was the main intended target but he was not there. He has not been seen since the shootings and may have fled the city in fear for his life. The FBI has so far been reluctant to get involved in bringing gangsters to justice but this latest outrage is certain to change all that. There are growing demands that Capone be brought down by Federal agents.

Illinoisans, meanwhile, are tiring of Prohibition, which has banned alcoholic beverages across America but also helped ruthless gangs get rich from illegal supplies.

One gang leader, Charlie Birger, was recently hanged after going to war against rivals in south Illinois. At one stage, the smuggler used armored "tanks" built from converted trucks to mount his attacks.

RAINBOW CITY, SHOWCASE FOR THE MODERN WORLD

By our technology editor
May 28, 1933

THE CENTURY of Progress International Exposition opened its gates to visitors in Chicago yesterday, delighting them with "dream cars" and "homes of tomorrow" among many futuristic exhibits.

The World's Fair, created to mark Chicago's first recognition as a town in 1833, is sited on over 400 acres of land along Lake Michigan's shore.

At a spectacular opening event last night, lights were activated when the star Arcturus was detected in the sky, chosen because its rays began their journey at about the same time as Chicago's previous World's Fair in 1893. The fairground buildings are multi-colored to create a "Rainbow City" in contrast to 1893's "White City." Visitors are moved around the site in special Greyhound buses.

The fair is a showcase for the latest advances in science and technology, particularly transport. Cadillac and Lincoln are unveiling their "dream cars" while railroad companies are exhibiting the new era of streamlined trains.

The popular "homes of tomorrow" displays suggest a future of dishwashers and air conditioning. The German "Graf Zeppelin," the world's largest airship, is scheduled to fly over Chicago, although it can expect a mixed reception. Many are unhappy with its association with German Chancellor Herr Adolf Hitler's controversial and brutal rise to power.

Nuclear Age dawns

AN ITALIAN-BORN physicist at the University of Chicago has created the world's first nuclear reactor, *writes our science correspondent, December 3, 1942.*

The Chicago Pile-1 research reactor, containing 45,000 graphite bricks and fueled by the radioactive element uranium, yesterday achieved a self-sustaining nuclear chain reaction that will go down in history as a major scientific breakthrough.

Until now, Mr. Enrico Fermi's work beneath the stands of the university's Stagg Field has been kept secret, and details remain understandably sketchy. He is thought to have tested atomic theory by splitting atoms, and has succeeded in releasing nuclear energy.

Awarded the Nobel Prize in Physics, Mr. Fermi left fascist-controlled Italy for the United States, and came to Chicago after accepting an earlier post at New York City's Columbia University.

According to friends, he has modestly described his reactor as a "crude pile of black bricks and wooden timbers."

Experts said last night that Mr. Fermi's breakthrough opened up the possibility of a world powered by cheap nuclear energy. But they also cautioned that his research could be used to develop nuclear weapons with the potential to destroy the planet.

Since entering World War II a year ago, the U.S., along with its Allies, is increasingly worried that Nazi Germany may be developing a nuclear weapon.

The Allies are racing to develop such a device first, and Mr. Fermi is certain to be at the heart of its development.

MIRACULOUS MOLDY MELON

MEDICINE FROM ROTTEN FRUIT SET TO SAVE ALLIED LIVES

By our science editor
October 1, 1943

A REVOLUTIONARY anti-bacterial drug is certain to become as indispensable to the Allied war effort as any weapon, U.S. military chiefs predicted yesterday. The fungus needed to mass-produce penicillin has been successfully isolated—from a moldy cantaloupe in a Peoria grocery store.

The discovery of penicillin by Scotsman Alexander Fleming more than a decade ago received limited attention at the time. However, World War II has since created an urgent need for antibacterials to combat diseases and infected wounds.

Finding the right fungus to make sufficient quantities has eluded scientists—until now. Thanks to the tireless work of the U.S. Department of Agriculture's research laboratory in Peoria, a "super mold" has been found capable of treating wounds as well as a wide range of life-threatening illnesses.

The ingenius Peoria scientists first tried to mass-produce penicillin using a syrupy by-product of cornstarch often dumped by local corn mills into the Illinois River. Although it upped the yield, they concluded that a more resilient mold was needed to maximize results.

Mycologist Kenneth Raper led the hunt for this tougher strain, ordering the U.S. Army Transport Command to collect new mold samples wherever they traveled in the world.

Peoria staff were also told to collect samples locally. Raper spent weeks sifting through decaying fruits, old cheeses, breads, meats, and soil samples, and finally came upon a mold on an overripe cantaloupe that was 50 times more potent than anything else previously tested.

It is said to have been brought in by a lab technician, now called "Moldy Mary." After cutting the precious mold off the rind, staff are understood to have sliced up the "miracle melon" and unceremoniously eaten it.

Military chiefs said yesterday the pharmaceutical industry was ready to begin producing millions of units of penicillin for the U.S., British, and other Allied armies. The antibacterial drug is expected to save many lives in wartime, and beyond.

They added that Nazi Germany's forces will have to rely on less effective sulfa drugs, which means higher fatalities and longer recovery times for their wounded.

WARTIME SPEECH FOR OUR TIMES

YOUNGSTERS BUY A PIECE OF HISTORY TO INSPIRE LEADERS OF TODAY

By our education editor
March 25, 1944

SCHOOL CHILDREN have proudly presented a rare copy of the Gettysburg Address written in President Lincoln's own hand to Illinois State officials at a ceremony in Springfield yesterday.

One of five hand-written copies of the speech, the President completed it at the request of Mr. Edward Everett, the former U.S. Secretary of State, who then sold it to help soldiers injured in the Civil War.

Thousands of Illinois children raised $50,000 to buy the "Everett copy" which had just become available. With jars sited in classrooms for collections, they donated an average of five cents apiece, often sacrificing their allowances. Mr. Marshall Field III, the department store heir, made up the remainder by donating $10,000.

The Gettysburg Address was

delivered by President Lincoln during the Civil War, at the dedication of the Soldiers' National Cemetery in Gettysburg, Pennsylvania.

As freedom and democracy are now under threat in a world war, its inspiring words—that government "of the people, by the people, for the people, shall not

perish from the earth"—are as relevant today as they were when first delivered in 1863. It seems

the children of Illinois have shown that they can appreciate these fine words just as well as any adult.

HIROSHIMA ATOM BOMB DROPPED BY QUINCY PILOT

By our war correspondent
August 7, 1945

THE ATOMIC BOMB that destroyed the Japanese city of Hiroshima yesterday was dropped from the B-29 Superfortress *Enola Gay*, piloted by Col. Paul Tibbets, born in

Japanese Americans, released from internment camps in the Pacific Coast area, flock to wartime Chicago, and are hired by companies desperate for labor. Many return to the Pacific Coast after WWII, but the Chicago community survives to this day.

Quincy, Illinois. The devastation caused by the single bomb called "Little Boy," dropped by Col. Tibbets and his crew, is so severe that exact casualty figures may never be known.

It is understood tens of thousands were killed in the explosion, and many more are certain to die as a result of their wounds, starvation or the new horror of war from atomic weapons—radiation poisoning.

Many of those killed or injured are believed to be civilians, although Hiroshima had a military garrison.

The nuclear attack was so overwhelming that military

chiefs believe it must surely compel Japan to surrender, which would bring to an end WWII following the collapse of Germany and Italy.

A Japanese surrender will avoid the need for Allied troops to mount what many predict would otherwise be an extremely bloody invasion of the country.

Col. Tibbets, who graduated from Alton's Western Military Academy, is among nearly one million Illinoisans who have served during World War II, of whom 22,000 have been killed.

The bomber, *Enola Gay*, was named by Col. Tibbets for his mother.

War heroes

ORCHARD Field Airport is renamed O'Hare International Airport in 1949, to honor the bravery of Edward "Butch" O'Hare, the Navy's WWII flying ace and Medal of Honor recipient, who later died in action.

Passengers will discover that boarding passes are still coded with the letters ORD—a throwback to Orchard Field.

Later, Silvis is home to Hero Street USA, famous for having more people serving in the military than any other comparable street in the nation.

Shining Temple to Tolerance Completed

A SPECTACULAR TEMPLE in Wilmette, Cook County, is being hailed as a modern wonder of Illinois after it was officially unveiled yesterday, *writes our religion correspondent, May 3, 1953.*

The Baha'i House of Worship was designed by the late Canadian architect Mr. Louis Bourgeois, and is the only such temple in the U.S. It is dedicated to a religion founded in Persia that teaches the unity of all major faiths.

Followers of the Baha'i faith around the world raised funds for the project. A model was displayed at the Chicago World's Fair.

The House of Worship took 30 years to construct, and is a domed structure finished in a special concrete mixture of cement and quartz that makes it shine white.

The building has nine entrances and nine sections, as in the Baha'i religion the number nine symbolizes absolute perfection.

It contains symbols from other major world religions including Christianity, Hinduism, and Buddhism—a "Temple to Tolerance."

During the turbulent decades in which it was built, wild rumors circulated including that the structure housed a live whale or perhaps served as a refueling station for captured German submarines.

Sadly, Mr. Bourgeois did not live to see his plans completed.

A SIGHT TO SHAME AMERICA

By our crime correspondent
September 5, 1955

EMMETT TILL has come home to Chicago, with thousands queuing to pay their respects over recent days at his public funeral.

The 14-year-old African American was murdered about a week ago while visiting relatives in the small rural town of Money in the southern state of Mississippi.

It is alleged that he was beaten and shot by store owner Roy Bryant and J. W. Milam, Bryant's half-brother. Emmett's body was later retrieved from the Tallahatchie River.

At the insistence of his mother, Mamie Till Bradley, her slain son's casket has been left open in order to show the world the brutality of his killing. "Let the people see

what they did to my boy!" she reportedly said.

Civil rights campaigners say his murder has focused attention on racism in America, and the issue of segregation.

Those who knew him said Emmett was like any other teenager and had led a happy life growing up on Chicago's South Side. He and his cousins and friends were known for their fun-loving natures, and would often pull pranks on each other.

Before his visit to the South, Emmett's mother had warned her son to take care because Chicago and Mississippi are two very different worlds.

His death has shocked all of America. Both the accused, Bryant and Milam, are expected to stand trial later this month. The court case promises to be one of the most highly publicized in recent times.

Prominent public figures including Chicago Mayor Richard J. Daley and Illinois Governor William Stratton have intervened to urge that justice must be done, and be seen to be done.

RIVER TURNS GREEN
CHICAGO HONORS IRISH SAINT

Big year for the Big Mac

WITH the nationwide launch of its "Big Mac" double-decker sandwich, McDonald's has had quite a year, *writes our business editor, December 31, 1968.*

Under the leadership of Ray Kroc, the company is on the path to becoming the world's most successful fast-food company. He has even established Hamburger University in Illinois to train McDonald's managers.

Born in Oak Park of Czech descent, Kroc once revealed he lied about his age in an attempt to drive a Red Cross ambulance at 15 in World War I. After WWII, he worked for the McDonald brothers who ran a small fast-food chain.

Kroc opened the first new-look McDonald's Corporation restaurant in Des Plaines, which proved a huge hit with diners.

He then franchised dozens of others but kept uniformity in quality and speedy service. By standardizing operations, he has succeeded in ensuring that every burger tastes the same in every restaurant.

In 1961, Kroc bought the company from the McDonald brothers, and is now expected to lead its global expansion.

By our culture editor
March 18, 1962

TO GASPS of delight from thousands of onlookers yesterday, the Chicago River was turned a startling emerald green as if by magic, a modern miracle in celebration of Ireland's patron saint.

Organized by the Chicago Journeymen Plumbers Local 130, it is the brainchild of Stephen Bailey, the union's business manager and chairman of the St. Patrick's Day Parade, the popular festival organized by the city's large community of Irish descendants.

City officials had previously been using traces of green dye to track waste being dumped in the river. Bailey then had the brainwave to turn all the river green to mark the festival.

Its temporary transformation is not without its problems. The organizers have reluctantly admitted that, if the greening of the river is to become an annual event, they will have to think again about the quantities of dye they use. They aim to reduce the 100 pounds they used yesterday, which is likely to last an entire week, to an amount that keeps the water green for no more than a day. Environmental campaigners are also warning that the dye chosen for the spectacle may be harming the river.

But in downtown yesterday, all the talk was about how it was done —not that Chicagoans are likely to find out the closely guarded secret. According to one organizer, revealing the formula would be like "telling where the leprechaun hides its gold."

Last man on the moon?

AN ASTRONAUT has walked on the barren surface of the moon for the last time—at least for the foreseeable future, *writes our space editor, December 15, 1972.*

Yesterday, Chicago-born astronaut Eugene "Gene" Cernan, the Apollo 17 commander, wrote his daughter's initials in the dust beside his own footprints. He then climbed back into the Lunar Module "Challenger" before setting off home.

Commander Cernan and his crewmates Harrison Schmitt and Ronald Evans are now safely on their way back to Earth.

Cernan is only the 11th person to step onto the surface of the moon, starting with Neil Armstrong, commander of the Apollo 11 mission in 1969.

He was fulfilling U.S. President John F. Kennedy's audacious 1961 goal of "landing a man on the moon and returning him safely to the

Earth" before the end of that decade. With the ending of the Apollo program in order to support the Skylab project, it is likely to be decades before anyone returns.

Former Boy Scout Cernan went to McKinley Elementary School in Bellwood followed by Proviso East High School in Maywood, and Purdue University. He served in the U.S. Navy as a pilot before being recruited by NASA to train as an astronaut.

REAGAN INAUGURATED

SON OF ILLINOIS BECOMES PRESIDENT OF AMERICA

By our politics editor
January 21, 1981

YESTERDAY WAS a day of pride for Illinoisans as "one of their own," Ronald Reagan, was inaugurated 40th President of the United States. He is the only President so far to be born in Illinois.

Growing up in small towns in the north of the State, his early life there made a deep and permanent impression on the boy who would one day be President.

Born into a poor family of Irish and English–Scots descent, the President at one time lived in a second floor apartment above a store in Tampico, the place where he was born. The family settled in Dixon where he attended high school, and became interested in acting and sports. He also served as a local lifeguard and is said to have rescued many people over six years on duty.

The young Reagan, nicknamed "Dutch" by his father, was strongly opposed to racial discrimination. When a local inn refused to let some African Americans stay, he took them home where his mother

invited them to spend the night.

He attended Eureka College, famous for the liberal arts, whose stated values are "learning, service, and leadership," and became student body president and captain of the swim team. After graduating, he worked as a

regional sports announcer for Chicago Cubs baseball games.

It was while traveling with the Cubs in California that the future President landed his first Hollywood role as an actor. He later married Nancy Davis, an actress who has lived in Chicago.

Despite his wealth of experience—he has also served as Governor of California—this "son of Illinois" has his critics. They predict he will struggle in the presidential role, though President Reagan is confident he will silence them all by growing the economy.

MYSTERY MOUNDS WERE GREAT CITY

ONCE A GIANT METROPOLIS—NOW A UNESCO WORLD HERITAGE SITE

By our archeology editor
December 18, 1982

EIGHTY MYSTERIOUS earthen mounds near East St. Louis and Collinsville were yesterday confirmed as a UNESCO World Heritage Site in recognition of their importance in the history of the Americas.

According to experts, the Native American settlement forming the Cahokia Mounds is the largest and most complex archeological site anywhere north of Mexico's ancient cities. At its peak in the 12th century, Cahokia's population has been estimated to be as high as 20,000, rivaling medieval London, usually considered to have been the largest city in the western world at that time.

Experts have established that the original site contained 120 mounds over a six-mile area, of which 80 remain. Monks Mound, said to be named for monks who lived there for a time, is the largest prehistoric earthwork in the Americas, and focal point of the sprawling city.

A grassy space near Monks Mound may have been used for games and rituals including "chunkey," which appears to have involved rolling a pill-shaped stone across the field. Men are thought to have thrown spears where they believed the stone would travel.

Experts remain baffled as to why the settlement was abandoned by the early 1300s, a common fate for ancient cities and the civilizations that built them.

One theory is that it declined after flooding; another, that it was invaded by rival peoples, or perhaps drought and famine caused the people to overthrow their leaders.

Cited by UNESCO as "a striking example of a complex chiefdom society," the Cahokia Mounds site is one of only 23 places in the U.S. to receive the prestigious World Heritage status.

IT'S GOLD YET AGAIN FOR A GREAT OLYMPIAN

By our athletics correspondent
August 3, 1992

EAST ST. LOUIS athlete Jackie Joyner-Kersee has joined the ranks of the all-time greats after winning gold at the Barcelona Olympics.

She triumphed in the heptathlon, which she also won along with gold in the long jump at the Seoul Olympics four years ago. Many regard the seven-event track-and-field contest as the ultimate challenge for any athlete. Named for JFK's wife Jackie Kennedy, Joyner-Kersee overcame severe asthma to pursue athletics at high school.

In 1986, and again the following year, she received the Jesse Owens Award, the nation's highest accolade given to outstanding track-and-field athletes.

According to many athletics commentators, her world records will remain difficult to surpass. She has come to dominate the heptathlon, which includes high jump, long jump, and the 100-meter hurdles.

Joyner-Kersee has established a foundation to help people obtain athletics lessons and improve their quality of life, particularly in East St. Louis.

Her brother, Al Joyner, also won gold in the triple jump at the 1984 Los Angeles Olympics.

SPORTING LEGEND RETIRES—AGAIN

THE WORLD'S greatest basketball player yesterday announced his retirement—for a second time, *writes our sports correspondent, January 14, 1999.*

Michael Jordan told a press conference at Chicago's United Center, home of the Chicago Bulls, that his playing days for the team he helped to achieve so much sporting success were finally over.

"My responsibilities have been to play the game of basketball and relieve some of the pressures of everyday life for people who work from nine to five. I've tried to do that to the best of my abilities," he said.

Jordan helped the Bulls win three NBA finals in a row before announcing his first retirement as a player.

Earlier, he won two Olympic golds —one in Los Angeles in 1984, and a second with the "Dream Team" in Barcelona eight years later.

Tragedy struck when his father was murdered, but to honor his dream of playing baseball, his son joined the Chicago White Sox minor league system.

In 1995, "His Airness" announced "I'm back," and rejoined the Bulls to win a second championship "three-peat."

Bulls chairman Jerry Reinsdorf said yesterday he hoped this moment would never come.

"This has to be the toughest day in the history of the Chicago Bulls... for basketball fans all over the world," he said.

OBAMA'S DONE IT!

ILLINOIS SENATOR ON HIS WAY TO THE WHITE HOUSE

By our politics editor
November 5, 2008

BARACK OBAMA last night became the first African American to be elected President, sweeping away the last racial barrier in U.S. politics with ease.

In jubilant scenes at Chicago's Grant Park, the President-Elect delivered a victory speech to inspire the nation.

Flanked by American flags, he declared to the jubilant 125,000 crowd: "If there is anyone out there who still doubts that America is a place where all things are possible, who still wonders if the dream of our founders is alive in our time, who still questions the power of our democracy, tonight is your answer."

He continued: "It's the answer told by lines that stretched around schools and churches in numbers this nation has never seen, by people who waited three hours and four hours, many for the first time in their lives, because they believed that this time must be different, that their voices could

be that difference. It's the answer spoken by young and old, rich and poor, Democrat and Republican, black, white, Hispanic, Asian, Native American, gay, straight, disabled, and not disabled."

Earlier, the Senator from Illinois and Democratic candidate had roundly defeated Republican rival John McCain, winning the presidency with 365 electoral votes to 173. He announced his candidacy for President more than a year ago in front of the Old State Capitol in Springfield where Abraham Lincoln made his famous "House Divided" speech. He went on to beat Chicago-born Hillary Clinton to win the Democratic nomination.

Mr. Obama, who taught law at the University of Chicago, fought a brilliant campaign that focused on hope and change, with an end to the Iraq war and reform of health care. With his entry into the White House, his Chicago-born wife Michelle becomes the nation's first African American First Lady.

On hearing the news of his victory, many spoke last night, of a new day dawning in U.S. politics.

African Americans said they had finally arrived in the "promised land" 40 years after Martin Luther King, Jr. said it was coming in his last speech before he was assassinated.

The world is celebrating along with America. Tomorrow has even been declared a holiday in Kenya, home of Mr. Obama's deceased father.

By our baseball editor
November 3, 2016

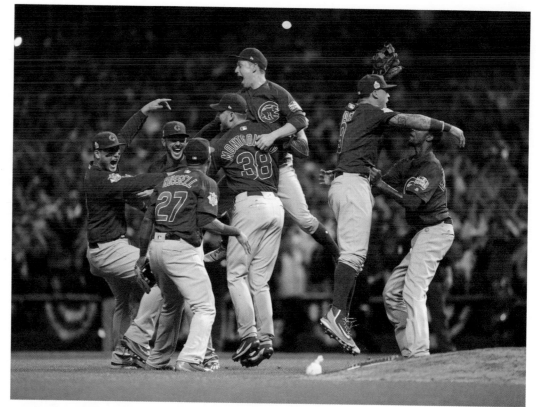

THE "Curse of the Cubs" is finally over after Chicago's "lovable losers" last night ended their 108-year World Series title drought in truly spectacular fashion. In an epic encounter, the Chicago Cubs overcame a 3–1 series deficit to beat the Cleveland Indians 4–3, and bring the Major League Baseball title back to Wrigley Field.

A thrilling Game 7 ended with thousands of Cubs fans crying tears of joy and waving their distinctive white flags with the team's blue "W" to signify a victory. "Do you believe in miracles?" read one fan's sign.

The "Curse of the Billy Goat" was broken last night, a curse dating back to the 1945 World Series when the final four games were played at Wrigley Field.

In game four of the series, local bar owner Billy Sianis arrived with two tickets, one for him and one for his goat. He was told to leave, and—according to legend—said the Cubs "ain't gonna win no more." The Cubs lost the series.

Last night the Cubs had to beat nearly 11 decades of gut-wrenching failure that had built a seemingly impossible wall of superstition between them and the title.

The Cubs' 1908 Series victory was their second in a row, the first time anyone had won it twice, and

CUBS' CURSE LIFTED
EPIC VICTORY ENDS 108 YEARS OF MISERY

the last of three consecutive years they had played in the Series, at the time a record for a major league team.

Few present at that time could have believed the Cubs' success would be followed by the longest ever world championship drought lasting more than a century.

A victory parade in Chicago is planned for the team, and the Chicago River may even be turned Cubs blue. For many, last night's triumph was an emotional affair as they remembered old friends and family who followed the Cubs in the dark days but have since passed away.

"I have waited my whole life for this," said one fan, crying tears of joy.

Grand Unveiling—*Tyrannosaurus rex* named Sue
MAY 17, 2000, FIELD MUSEUM OF NATURAL HISTORY, CHICAGO, ILLINOIS

Guest of honor—Paleontologist Susan Hendrickson, discoverer of *T. rex* Sue in South Dakota.

- A show 65 million years in the making
- Survivor of geological ages (and five years of bitter legal controversy)
- The biggest and most complete *T. rex* yet found
- $7.6 million—the most expensive fossil in history
- The dinosaur with the coolest name ever!

Logo For Illinois' 200th Birthday Party

A SPECIALLY DESIGNED Illinois Bicentennial logo to celebrate the State's 200th birthday was unveiled in Springfield by Governor Bruce Rauner yesterday, *writes our state correspondent, January 13, 2017*.

The logo is a centerpiece of the Bicentennial celebrations to mark Illinois' entry to the Union as the 21st State two centuries ago. It is hoped the logo will be used on flags flown from state and other public buildings in Illinois from the start of 2018, 200 years since it achieved statehood.

Designed by Ben Olson, the gold-and-blue logo depicts an outline of the State surrounded by 21 stars. In the middle is a gold-colored "200" in a white sunburst, its rays spreading in all directions to suggest the impact Illinois has made in the country and the world over the past two centuries, as well as its bright future ahead.

"We reflect virtually every aspect of America. We are a crossroads of the nation," said Governor Rauner.

The logo follows a special centennial flag designed by Wallace Rice in 1918 to mark Illinois' first 100 years.

BICENTENNIAL OF STATEHOOD
LAND OF LINCOLN MARKS ITS PLACE IN AMERICAN HISTORY

By our history editor
January 1, 2018

ILLINOIS TODAY begins a year-long celebration of the 200th anniversary of its entry to the Union as the 21st State.

The Bicentennial will see a host of events take place across Illinois, enabling communities in cities, towns, and rural areas to take pride in their State. Many public buildings are expected to fly an official Bicentennial flag that depicts Illinois as the "crossroads of the nation."

There is much to celebrate: Illinois is rightly proud of being home to no less than three illustrious U.S. Presidents: Abraham Lincoln, Ulysses S. Grant, and Barack Obama. A fourth—Ronald Reagan—was born and raised there. The State honors Lincoln with its official slogan, adopted in 1955: "Land of Lincoln."

Illinois has led the way in agriculture, transport, food-processing, engineering, technology—including the development of the web browser—commerce, architecture, sport, and culture, and has been at the forefront of the anti-slavery movement and votes for women.

Today, with 12 million people, Illinois is America's fifth most populous state. Its multi-cultural, ethnically diverse citizens include many of German, Irish, Polish, and Swedish descent. There are large African American, Latino, Asian American, Jewish and Muslim communities.

The State boasts some of America's best farmland—a major producer of corn, soybeans, meat, and even pumpkins — and has been a pioneer of nuclear energy. The University of Chicago and other educational institutions rank among the best.

Chicago, Illinois' largest city and America's third most populous, is an economic powerhouse and one of the world's most important business centers, led by the Board of Trade and Mercantile Exchange. It thrives as a transport hub for rail and air—O'Hare International is among the world's busiest airports.

For many, Illinois and its Chicago metropolis will always be the "beating heart of America." What will its legacy be for the next 200 years?

A TIMELINE GUIDE TO
THE HISTORY OF ILLINOIS

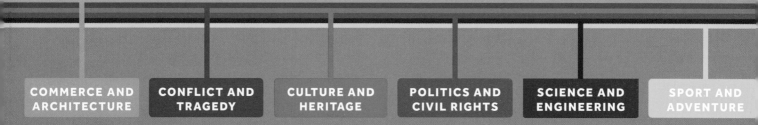

| COMMERCE AND ARCHITECTURE | CONFLICT AND TRAGEDY | CULTURE AND HERITAGE | POLITICS AND CIVIL RIGHTS | SCIENCE AND ENGINEERING | SPORT AND ADVENTURE |

HOW TO USE THE TIMELINE

Unfold the pages of *The Illinois Chronicles* to travel through time on a remarkable 200-year-long journey, from the birth of the Prairie State to the present day. Each colored line represents a different theme in the story. A selection of key moments in U.S. history also helps highlight the important role Illinois has played in national events and beyond.

On the back of the timeline you will find a map of the State showing top places to visit, Illinois and Chicago flags, and an Illinois Honor Roll. There is also a useful glossary to guide you through some of the concepts mentioned in *The Illinois Chronicles* timeline.

It all adds up to an amazing story of people and events whose unique legacy can still be felt today in the 21st State of the Union.

ILLINOIS
1818-2018

1832
BLACK HAWK leads Sauk and other Native Americans from Iowa across the Mississippi River into Illinois, battling soldiers and frontier militia. Black Hawk's defeat encourages more European immigrants to settle in the State. A young Abraham Lincoln serves in the militia.

1840
GERMAN AND
escaping confl
establish comm
Illinois. Earlier,
founded by Ne
many of Purita
Italian, and Sw
will see the po
million in 20 ye
Arthur their ho

1818
ILLINOIS, the French name for local Native Americans, becomes the 21st State with the Mississippi and Ohio rivers as boundaries. The **Prairie State** gets land where the city of Chicago will later grow up, giving access to the Atlantic and the world through Lake Michigan.

★

U.S. EXPANSION
A TREATY IN 1819 fixes the boundary between the United States and New Spain, adding to lands from the Mississippi to the Rocky Mountains bought from France in the Louisiana Purchase of 1803. In 1848, following victory in the Mexican–American war, the U.S. will seize territory stretching from Texas to the Pacific Ocean. Alaska will be bought from Russia in 1867. Hawaii will enter the Union as the 50th state in 1959.

1837
BLACKSMITH **JOHN DEERE** makes a moldboard plow from a steel saw, thus solving the problem of farming sticky Midwest soil only a year after he arrives in Illinois from New England. His business will later move to Moline and grow to be a world leader in agricultural machinery and services.

1839
THE **TRAIL OF TEARS** claims the lives of thousands of Cherokees from Georgia, forced to relocate west of the Mississippi under an army escort in winter. Crossing southern Illinois, the bitter cold and snow bring their trek to a near standstill, causing many deaths.

1818
KASKASKIA, a former French town, briefly serves as the first **state capital**. Its "Liberty Bell of the West"—a gift from Louis XV to a local church—was rung during the Revolutionary War. Today the town has a tiny population, the original settlement having been destroyed by flooding.

1810s **1820s** **1830s** **1840s**

1818
ALBION IS CREATED as an ideal farming society, part of the 26,000-acre "English Settlement" founded by sheep breeders and idealists George Flower and Morris Birkbeck. Their "**utopia**" is famous for its advanced agriculture and rejection of slavery, but declines after the pair quarrel.

1819
VANDALIA becomes the new **state capital** until 1839. How Vandalia, a terminus of the **National Road**, gets its name is uncertain, but one mischievous theory is city leaders mistakenly and bizarrely think Vandals, an ancient Germanic tribe, are actually Native Americans.

1837
CHICAGO wins city status. It has grown from a tiny settlement founded by Jean Baptiste Point DuSable—said to be from Haiti of African and French descent—on lands of the Potawatomi people. The city's name is possibly the Native American word for the wild onions or garlic found in local marshes.

1837
ELIJAH LOVEJOY, campaigning journalist and anti-slavery newspaper editor, leaves slave-state Missouri for Illinois after his printing presses are repeatedly smashed, but is murdered by a mob in Alton attacking his new press. He will be considered the "first casualty" of the Civil War.

1840
MORMON FO
Smith rename
Commerce "N
followers sett
be murdered i
accused of or
destruction of
premises. In 2
apologize for
Mormons and

1
T a
it
A V
v
t b
b
s
c

★

RAILROADS
IN 1825 JOHN STEVENS builds a test track and runs a locomotive on it in New Jersey. The Baltimore and Ohio railroad will start a transport revolution, replacing canals. America's railroad network grows rapidly. By 1916 trackage will be 230,500 miles, nearly equivalent to 10 times round the Earth.

KEY

SPORT AND ADVENTURE	CONFLICT AND TRAGEDY
SCIENCE AND ENGINEERING	COMMERCE AND ARCHITECTURE
CULTURE AND HERITAGE	POLITICS AND CIVIL RIGHTS

★ **U.S. NATIONAL HISTORY MOMENTS**

See back of Timeline for useful **Glossary** and Illinois Honor Roll

Jane Addams
1860–1935

Founder of Chicago's Hull-House social experiment, leading social activist and suffragist.

Ida B. Wells
1862–1931

African American journalist, civil rights campaigner, and campaigner for votes for women.

Grace Wilbur Trout
1864–1955

Played a leading role in the campaign to allow women in Illinois to vote for U.S. President, and then all elections.

Frank Lloyd Wright
1867–1959

Considered America's greatest architect, leader of the Prairie style of architecture.

Robert Sengstacke Abbott 1870–1940

African American lawyer, editor, and publisher of the *Chicago Defender* newspaper.

Carl Sandburg
1878–1967

Poet and writer who won a Pulitzer Prize for his biography of Abraham Lincoln, and two more for poetry.

Cyrus Tang
1930–

Businessman whose philanthropy extends to a UChicago research center and the Field Museum's Hall of China.

Sandra Cisneros
1954–

The Chicago-born Hispanic American bestselling author is today a key figure in Chicana literature.

Oprah Winfrey
1954–

Television host, media mogul, philanthropist, and one of America's most influential people.

Barack Obama
1961–

U.S. Senator from Illinois and the 44th U.S. President, the first African American to hold that great office.

Jackie Joyner-Kersee
1962–

One of the world's greatest ever track-and-field athletes, specializing in the long jump and heptathlon.

Michael Jordan
1963–

Considered by many the greatest basketball player ever, and the first African American owner of an NBA team.

WITH GRATEFUL THANKS TO OUR PARTNERS:

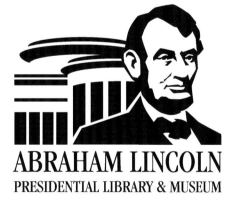

THANKS ALSO TO:

Chicago History Museum
Harold Washington Library Center/Chicago Public Library
Chicago Cultural Center
Museum of Science and Industry, Chicago
Chicago Architecture Foundation
Smithsonian Institution, Washington, D.C.

Ulysses S. Grant
1822–1885

Commanding General of the U.S. Army in the Civil War and 18th President of the United States.

Marshall Field
1834–1906

Department store tycoon, philanthropist for whom the Field Museum of Natural History is named.

Aaron Montgomery
Ward 1844–1913

Made a fortune through his mail-order company; a tireless campaigner for Chicago and its people.

Daniel Burnham
1846–1912

The architect and city planner, and director of works for the acclaimed World's Columbian Exposition in Chicago.

Augustus Tolton
1854–1897

Formerly enslaved, he is the first publicly acknowledged African American Roman Catholic priest in the U.S.

"W. D." Boyce
1858–1929

Publisher, explorer, supporter of workers' rights, and founder of the Boy Scouts of America.

Ronald Reagan
1911–2004

33rd Governor of California and then served two terms as 40th President of the U.S.

Muddy Waters
1913–1983

McKinley Morganfield, hugely admired musician hailed as the father of modern electric blues.

Harry Caray
1914–1998

Sportscaster, famed for "Take Me Out to the Ball Game" sung at Chicago White Sox and Cubs home games.

Paul Tibbets
1915–2007

United States pilot who dropped the first atomic bomb used in war on the city of Hiroshima in Japan.

Harold Washington
1922–1987

Lawyer and politician who served as Mayor of Chicago, the first of African American descent.

Fazlur Rahman Khan
1929–1982

Born in present-day Bangladesh, designer of Chicago's John Hancock Center and Willis (Sears) Tower.

Mormons Members of the Church of Jesus Christ of Latter-day Saints, who believe in the Bible but also other scriptures, such as the Book of Mormon.

National Road The first major U.S. highway built by the federal government that becomes a main transport route for western settlers.

Paleontologist A scientist who searches for and studies fossils to determine everything about an organism, how it evolved and what the environment it lived in was like.

Penicillin A group of antibiotics among the first medications to be effective against many bacterial infections, most of which had been untreatable and a major cause of death.

Philanthropist A person who is led by their love for fellow human beings to make a gift, usually of money, to promote others' well-being or support an organization or institution that is dedicated to doing so.

Prairie State A popular alternative name for the State of Illinois because so much of it was prairie, temperate grass, and shrub lands that made excellent farmland and also formed a huge swath across many U.S. states.

Prairie style A specifically Midwest style of architecture developed by some late 19th- and early 20th-century architects, and showcased in grand homes, typically comprising low-angled roofs, stained-glass windows, and high levels of craftsmanship.

Second Chicago School A new wave of architects in the 1940s and 1970s whose designs include new building technologies such as tube-frame structures for skyscrapers.

Settlement movement Social reformers in America and Britain who seek to get the prosperous and poor to live closer together in inter-dependent communities, sharing knowledge and culture in "settlement houses" located in poor urban areas.

State capital Not necessarily a state's biggest city but that chosen or built to be its seat of government.

State Capitol Not to be confused with "state capital," this is the building where the state legislative body meets.

Trail of Tears One of a series of forced removals of Native Americans from their homelands in the southeast of the U.S. to designated areas west of the Mississippi River.

Underground Railroad A 19th-century network of secret routes and safe houses set up to help people escape slavery by fleeing to U.S. free states and Canada.

Utopia An ideal society whose members live in harmony, often based on equality in government and justice, as described in the 1516 book *Utopia* by English statesman Thomas More.

World War I Considered the first global war. Rivalries between European powers spark conflict in 1914. Britain, France, and their allies fight against Germany and the Austro-Hungarian and Ottoman empires. Incensed by German actions, including the sinking of her ships, America joins the fighting in 1917. Germany and her allies surrender in 1918.

POLISH families,
t in Europe,
unities across
Rockford is
Englanders,
descent. Irish,
dish immigrants
ulation soar to 2
rs. **Amish** make
e.

1851
A LAND GRANT allows work to begin on the Illinois Central Railroad, lobbied for by Senator Stephen Douglas and future President Abraham Lincoln. The "Main Line of Mid-America" from Cairo to Galena has a branch to Chicago, sealing the city's success as a major transportation hub.

1861
MARY TODD from Kentucky had earlier married Abraham Lincoln in Springfield. As First Lady in Washington, D.C., she becomes a tragic figure, suffering depression after President Lincoln's assassination and the loss of three of four sons. She will be briefly committed to an asylum.

1865
THE UNION STOCK Yard is built on swampland by railroad companies, and will become the center of America's meatpacking industry after overtaking Cincinnati. The yard will become a tourist stop and even get a mention in a Frank Sinatra song, "My Kind Of Town."

1
A
W
Ch
Ar
cr
Re
M
by
fr
ch

1847
CYRUS McCORMICK opens a Chicago factory to make his invention of a revolutionary mechanical reaper for Midwest farmers. It will sell worldwide. He will exhibit the machine at London's Crystal Palace, and will be awarded the French Legion of Honor for services to world agriculture.

1848
SLAVERY IS BANNED in Illinois after previously being tolerated in parts of the State, but African Americans from other states are barred from residing here. Quincy and Chester, part of the **Underground Railroad**, help people escaping slavery to U.S. "**free states**" and Canada.

1861
CAIRO, once visited by famed novelist Charles Dickens, plays a vital part in the American Civil War. It is here in "**Little Egypt**" that the Mississippi and Ohio rivers meet, and it will be an important base for Union supplies, troops, and their commanding officer, Ulysses S. Grant.

1868
A NEW GRAND **Stat**
Capitol is funded by
growing prosperity. It
20 years to complete.
in the French Renaiss
style, the Springfield
government will be ta
than the U.S. Capitol
Washington, D.C., its
covered in gleaming

1850s

1860s

1870

846
E ILLINOIS-BASED Donner
d Reed families, believing
s Manifest Destiny that
erica should colonize the
est, head for California by
gon train. They are forced
winter in the Sierra Nevada,
their food runs out and
ne are said to resort to
nibalism.

1858
ABRAHAM LINCOLN, charismatic lawyer and politician, wins a national reputation after making a speech in the third state capital of Springfield. He warns that expanding slavery in the new U.S. territories is a threat to the Union: "A house divided against itself cannot stand."

1864
ULYSSES S. GRANT of Galena is appointed as the U.S. Army's Civil War commander and will accept Confederate commander Robert E. Lee's surrender at Appomattox in 1865. Galena's residents give him a house, and he will be elected U.S. President twice to help re-build the nation.

NDER JOSEPH
the town of
uvoo" after his
there. Smith will
a Carthage jail,
ering the
ewspaper
4, Illinois will
pelling the early
lling Smith.

1848
A BRAND NEW waterway links the Great Lakes and the Mississippi making Chicago center of a huge waterborne transport system. The 96-mile Illinois and Michigan Canal crosses the Chicago Portage where Native Americans and French explorers had needed to carry their canoes.

★

AMERICAN CIVIL WAR
THE BLOODIEST WAR in U.S. history starts in 1861 after 11 Southern States secede from the Union fearing new President Abraham Lincoln will curtail slavery, on which their economy is built. Lincoln issues the Emancipation Proclamation in 1863. The war ends two years later with the Union restored and slavery ended, but Lincoln is assassinated, and the South is devastated by war.

1865
AFRICAN AMERICAN John Jones leads a movement to repeal the discriminatory "black laws" shortly after the State becomes the first to ratify the 13th Amendment, which abolishes slavery.

1871
THE GR
starts i
but spr
17,500
people
homele
one of
to surv
a leadi
will ris

1894
PULLMAN RAIL CAR workers strike as their wages—but not rents—are cut in their "company town" of Pullman. They call for a boycott of Pullman's rail cars but, despite causing disruption, the strike collapses. President Cleveland, however, will make Labor Day a national holiday.

1899
ERNEST HEMINGWAY is born in Oak Park. He will excel in English at school, get wounded driving WWI ambulances, and write the Spanish Civil War novel *For Whom The Bell Tolls*. In 1954 the celebrated war correspondent and author will be awarded the Nobel Prize in Literature.

1902
MARSHALL FIELD'S new department store opens in Chicago. Field will be famous for the sayings, "Give the lady what she wants" and "The customer is always right." As a **philanthropist**, he will help fund the Field Museum of Natural History and the University of Chicago.

1910
W. D. BOYCE, millionaire publisher and explorer, goes on to found the Boy Scouts of America, inspired by the retired British general Robert Baden-Powell, author of the manual *Scouting for Boys*. Scouting will grow to be one of the United States' largest youth movements.

1901
THE **PRAIRIE STYLE** is developed by Chicago-based architect **Frank Lloyd Wright**, inspired by Midwest landscapes. He will be acclaimed by many as the nation's finest architect, and his domestic masterpieces will include Springfield's Dana-Thomas House and Chicago's Robie House.

1907
SEARS CATALOG FLOURISHES under Julius Rosenwald's leadership. The Chicago-based mail-order book becomes a consumers' bible, especially for rural customers, selling everything from sewing machines and automobiles to ready-to-assemble kit houses. Its "Wish Book" is famous for Christmas toys and gifts.

1912
TARZAN OF THE APES created by Chicago-b[orn] author **Edgar Rice Bur[roughs]**. Many books and films follow. Best known for him will be Johnny We[issmuller,] Olympic swimming cha[mpion] and childhood polio su[fferer] whose family settle in [...] from central Europe.

1895
"MURDER CASTLE" proprietor H. H. HOLMES is convicted of the single killing of an associate but confesses to dozens more. The medical graduate's Chicago hotel has secret doors and chambers to help him slay staff and guests, and conceal his crimes. Holmes will be hanged in 1896.

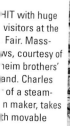

1900s

1910s

COLUMBIAN [...] hicago marks [...] Christopher [...] al in the New [...] s construction [...] city planner [...] m, and has [...] dings, the [...] r Ferris wheel, [...] sitors.

1896
ORPHAN "BILLY" SUNDAY signs for the Chicago White Stockings. He will convert to Christianity, end his baseball career, and become a popular evangelist—enemy of the "evil" liquor trade. He will later be immortalized in "Chicago," the song made famous by Frank Sinatra.

1900
THE CHICAGO RIVER has its flow permanently reversed so that water from Lake Michigan flushes sewage and factory waste into the new Chicago Sanitary and Ship Canal. The engineering triumph is achieved with a series of locks, and curbs the diseases that had plagued the city.

1903
THE IROQUOIS THEATRE Fire claims 600 lives, the deadliest single-building fire in U.S. history. Theater-goers, many of them children, struggle to find exits after a light ignites a curtain. The tragedy leads to safety improvements such as exit door "panic bars," saving many lives around the world.

1913
WOMEN WIN TH[E ...] Illinois, the first [...] Mississippi whe[re ...] but they cannot [...] Governor, only U[.S. ...] use the same ba[llot ...] The partial victor[y ...] campaign led by [... Grace Wilbur] **Trout** across Illi[nois ...] rights will come in [...]

1905
THE CHICAGO DEFENDER newspaper is founded by African American lawyer **Robert Sengstacke Abbott**, and gains national readership. It campaigns against racist "**Jim Crow laws**" and for the "Great Migration" of African Americans from the South to the North in search of jobs.

⭐ **THE GREAT MIGRATION**

DESPITE the abolition of slavery, the "Jim Crow laws" condemn African Americans in the South to segregation, rural poverty, and injustice. America entering WWI in 1917 boosts industry but creates labor shortages. More than 6 million head north and west for jobs but tensions provoke race riots.

HIT with huge [...] visitors at the [...] Fair. Mass- [...] ws, courtesy of [...] heim brothers' [...] and. Charles [...] of a steam- [...] n maker, takes [...] th movable

1900
THE WONDERFUL WIZARD of Oz is introduced to the world in the children's book by L. Frank Baum, first published in Chicago. The Grand Opera House will stage a musical version, and the 1939 movie will be one of cinema's greatest. It will become a key part of American culture.

FLAGS AND GOVERNMENT

FLAG OF ILLINOIS (1915)

A contest to create a state flag is won by Lucy Derwent Keeler, of the Daughters of the American Revolution Rockford chapter. Her design depicts the Great Seal of Illinois, the state emblem seen on many official documents. In 1970 the Illinois name is added after a petition from a Vietnam serviceman who says many do not recognize the flag.

FLAG OF CHICAGO (1917)

Wallace Rice designs one of America's most distinctive flags. Five blue and white stripes represent Chicago features including the two great waters that meet there. Rice's flag contains just two stars representing the Great Fire and World's Fair. In 1933 a third is added for the Century of Progress Exposition. A fourth later symbolizes Fort Dearborn. A fifth may yet be added to mark the 1968 Special Olympics, held in Chicago.

FLAG OF COOK COUNTY (1961)

Named after Daniel Pope Cook, an early Illinois statesman, the county is among the most populous in the U.S. as it includes much of metropolitan Chicago. It is thought to be one of the first counties to have its own flag—white with "Cook County" in large letters. In the center is part of a seal adopted in 1960 after a contest among school pupils. It depicts a map of the county, the date of its creation in 1831, and a circle of stars for each of the 38 historic townships, plus Chicago.

ILLINOIS CENTENNIAL FLAG (1918)

To mark its first 100 years, Wallace Rice, creator of Chicago's flag, designs a centennial flag for Illinois. It has three white and blue bands and 21 stars—10 blue in the upper white band and 10 in the lower, representing the 20 States at the time of Illinois' entry to the Union. At the center is a large white star for Illinois itself.

ILLINOIS BICENTENNIAL FLAG (2018)

Designed by Ben Olson, the flag's gold-and-blue logo picks up on Illinois as "crossroads of the nation." Marking its entry to the Union as the 21st State, an outline of Illinois is surrounded by 21 stars. In the middle is a gold-colored "200" in a white sunburst, its rays spreading in all directions to suggest the impact Illinois has made in the country and the world over the past two centuries, as well as its bright future ahead.

GREAT SEAL OF THE STATE OF ILLINOIS

Designed in 1819, the official emblem of the state depicts a banner in an eagle's beak containing the motto "State Sovereignty, National Union." A new seal is adopted in 1868 with a banner that twists. It is said that after the American Civil War and because Abraham Lincoln made Illinois his home, the banner's motto now appears to emphasize "National Union" over "State Sovereignty."

CONSTITUTION OF ILLINOIS

Illinois is governed by a written Constitution, its fourth and current version dating from 1970. The first Constitution in 1818 is the result of a convention held to draft it, where slavery is prohibited throughout most—but not all—of the State. Two more Constitutions follow in the 19th century. The latest one includes "home rule" powers for larger municipalities and other units of local government, and the creation of a state board of education. Like the U.S. Bill of Rights, its Bill of Rights protects freedom of speech, religion, and assembly. It also deals with discrimination based on race, sex, physical or mental handicaps.

GOVERNMENT OF ILLINOIS

The State has three branches of state government:

Executive

The Governor is elected for four years, and is in charge of many departments, boards, agencies, and commissions. Among the Governor's responsibilities are the supervision of the state police, state-wide transportation, and helping to further the Illinois economy.

Legislative

State laws are made by the General Assembly comprising 118 members of the House of Representatives, each elected to two-year terms, and 59 members of the Senate, whose terms typically are four years. They meet in the Illinois State Capitol in Springfield.

Judicial

The judiciary is composed of the seven elected members of the Supreme Court of Illinois as well as lesser courts that deal with criminal and civil cases. The Supreme Court rules on constitutional matters affecting the State.

Local government

In addition to state government, Illinois has more counties, cities, townships, villages, and districts than any other U.S. State. Many of them enjoy "home rule" powers that allow them to issue local laws or codes.

U.S. government

The powers of the federal government—originally created for collective defence of the States and foreign diplomacy—are placed in the President, Congress, and the U.S. Supreme Court in a system of "checks and balances." Congress has 435 elected members of the House of Representatives —18 from Illinois—and 100 elected members of the Senate, two from each of the 50 States.

ILLINOIS HONOR ROLL

Elijah Parish Lovejoy
1802–1837

Outspoken anti-slavery journalist and Presbyterian minister murdered by pro-slavery mob.

John Deere
1804–1886

Inventor and founder of one of the world's leading agricultural equipment manufacturers.

Abraham Lincoln
1809–1865

Leader of the North in the Civil War, and considered by many to be the greatest ever U.S. President.

Cyrus McCormick
1809–1884

Businessman and inventor of the first successful mechanical reaper, revolutionizing farming.

Lydia Moss Bradley
1816–1908

Peoria-based philanthropist, the first woman on a national bank board, and founder of Bradley University.

Mary Lincoln
1818–1882

Tragic First Lady of the U.S., and later the deeply traumatized widow of President Lincoln.

Bessie Coleman
1892–1926

Acknowledged as the first woman pilot of African American and Native American descent.

George Halas
1895–1983

Inspirational founder and owner of the Chicago Bears, and co-founder of the National Football League.

Ernest Hemingway
1899–1961

Writer and adventurer who captured the human experience of the troubled first half of the 20th century.

Enrico Fermi
1901–1954

Physicist credited as one of the architects of both the atomic bomb and the nuclear age.

Richard J. Daley
1902–1976

Mayor of Chicago for 21 years, who played a major role in Democratic politics; a key supporter of John F. Kennedy.

Ray Kroc
1902–1984

Businessman who built McDonald's into the world's most successful fast-food corporation, and made a fortune.

GLOSSARY

American Dream A national ideal that no matter where a person must start, anything is possible in this "land of the free."

Amish A traditionalist Christian community, known for simple living, plain dress, and avoidance of modern technology, where possible.

Anarchists Anti-authority political activists who believe all organized government is wrong and oppose it, sometimes violently.

Baha'i A religious faith founded in Persia that teaches unity—of humanity and all major religions—and the existence of one God as the source of all creation.

Chicago School Not an academic school but a group of architects who share many of the same ideas on how buildings should be designed and are among the first to adopt new construction technologies in commercial buildings.

Choreographed Dance moves artistically composed and arranged to go with music.

Company town A model community comprising housing and stores built and owned by a neighborhood's main employer who rents homes to its own staff.

Constitution An outline of basic principles that a nation, state or other organization is acknowledged to be governed by, and forms the basis of its laws and government.

Draft dodgers Those who illegally, or by exploiting loopholes in the system, avoid joining the armed forces when eligible and selected to do so.

Franchise The right to use a company's business model and brand, sold or bought for a fixed period of time.

Free state A state in the United States in which slavery is banned or being legally phased out before 1865 when it is abolished throughout the U.S.

Gettysburg Address A great speech by President Lincoln during the American Civil War at the dedication of the Soldiers' National Cemetery in Gettysburg, Pennsylvania.

Improv comedy A form of cabaret theater in which comedians perform without the use of a prepared written script.

Jim Crow laws State and local laws used to enforce racial segregation after the abolition of slavery by the national government throughout the Union in 1865. Jim Crow was an insulting term for African Americans.

Land grant A gift of public land made by a government to enable works such as railroads to be undertaken, said to be justified because the projects are in the public interest.

Little Egypt A distinct area of southern Illinois bordered by rivers—the Mississippi, Ohio, Wabash, Kaskaskia, and Little Wabash —that may derive its name from similarities to Egypt's Nile Delta.

Manhattan Project A top-secret team of U.S. and Allied scientists and engineers who carried out research for and built the first nuclear weapons, known as atomic bombs, during WWII.

Manifest Destiny The 19th century belief that it is inevitable and desirable that the United States expand to include all lands between the Atlantic and Pacific Oceans, which means taking land by necessity from Native Americans, Mexico, and beyond.

1876

WINDY CITY, Chicago's
famous nickname, is probably
first used as an insult by
newspapers in Cincinnati, its
sport and meatpacking rival.
Later, critics of Chicago's
bid for a World's Fair are
said to have used the phrase
to suggest its citizens are
boasters.

1886

"CAP" STREETER'S steamboat
gets stuck on a sandbar off
Chicago's north shore. He
claims it as independent
territory, invites builders to
dump rubble there, and issues
deeds to "homesteaders."
However, his ownership of
valuable "Streeterville" is
rejected in court.

1892

CHICAGO'S RAPID TRANSIT
system, America's second
oldest, is called the "L"
because much of the network
is "elevated." Its lines
cannot enter the central
business district, but in 1897
property owners will finally
be persuaded to let the Loop
encircle the area.

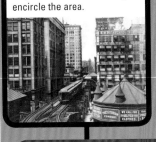

1876

"WILD BILL" HICKOK,
legendary gunfighter and
showman raised in LaSalle
County, is shot and killed while
playing poker in Deadwood,
the gold-rush town of Dakota
Territory. The cards he had
been dealt, aces and eights,
will later be named the "dead
man's hand."

1886

AUGUSTUS TOLTON, born
enslaved in Missouri, becomes
the first African American
Catholic priest in America. He
ministers in Quincy, his home
parish, and will develop
Chicago's St Monica's as an
African American "national
parish church." He is in the
process of being made a saint.

1887

A NEW TYPE of baseball
with a larger ball is invented
in Chicago. Officially called
"Softball" in the 1920s, it
is sometimes described as
"ladies' baseball"—although
women have been paid to
play baseball itself in front of
paying crowds since a game
in Springfield in 1875.

1892

IDA B. WELLS, born into
slavery in Mississippi, wins
fame as an African American
journalist—detailing lynching
in the South—and Civil Rights
campaigner. Later, she will
settle in Chicago and work to
improve conditions for the
city's growing African
American community.

1880s

1890s

1876

PRESIDENT LINCOLN'S BODY
is saved from a gang who
attempt to steal it from his
tomb in Oak Ridge Cemetery,
and hold it for ransom. In
1865 his coffin had been
transported by train 1,600
miles from Washington, D.C.,
to Springfield, past thousands
of grief-stricken onlookers.

1886

THE HAYMARKET RIOT follows
a Chicago workers' rally after
a bomb is thrown at police.
Of eight convicted
anarchists, only one may
have been directly involved.
Despite this, four are hanged.
Three are later pardoned by
German-born Governor John
Peter Altgeld.

1889

JANE ADDAMS co-founds
Hull-House in a poor district of
Chicago, with a night school,
clubs for children, and a
research center. Pioneer of
social work and the
Settlement Movement, this
"mother to the nation" will
be awarded the Nobel Peace
Prize in 1931.

1893

THE WORL
Exposition
400 years s
Columbus'
World. The
is overseer
Daniel Bu
around 200
world's firs
and 27 mil

1879

LOUIS SULLIVAN joins
Dankmar Adler to lead the
"**Chicago School**" or
"Commercial style" of
architecture. With other
architects in the city, they will
design grand offices and retail
stores. A "**Second Chicago
School**" in structural design
will later emerge.

1885

A SKYSCRAPER, said to be the
world's first, rises from the ashes
as architects and engineers
rebuild Chicago after the Great
Fire. Supported by a giant
frame using iron and steel,
William LeBaron Jenney's
10-story Home Insurance
Building will inspire cities
around the world.

1891

THE CHICAGO SYMPHONY
Orchestra is formed by German-
born conductor Theodore
Thomas and will become one of
America's "Big Five" orchestras.
Its South Michigan Avenue home
will host classical concerts by
world-class performers.
Conductors will include Aaron
Copland, Edward Elgar, Richard
Strauss, and Daniel Barenboim.

1893

POPCORN
amounts s
Chicago V
productio
the city's
Cracker J
Cretors, in
powered
to the stre
wagons.

1916

NAVY PIER on Lake Michigan is built for freight and passenger traffic, but will serve as a temporary jail for **World War I draft dodgers**. It will be named "Navy Pier" in 1927 in honor of naval veterans. Later, it will attract millions of visitors every year as Chicago's top tourist stop.

1917

WALT DISNEY is school cartoonist at McKinley High, Chicago, drawing WWI scenes. He will take night courses at the Art Institute of Chicago, and join the Red Cross. He will create animated movie stars including Mickey Mouse, Snow White, and the Seven Dwarfs.

★
PROHIBITION

THE 18TH AMENDMENT, and the Volstead Act that makes it an enforceable law from 1920, bans alcoholic beverages in a bid to curb crime and poverty. Federal agents try to enforce the law but organized crime gangs make fortunes from their trade in illegal supplies. Prohibition will finally be ended in 1933.

1925

THE TRI-STATE Tornado is the worst in U.S. history—claiming 695 lives—a mile-wide storm smashing towns along its track through Missouri, Illinois, and Indiana. Murphysboro loses 234 residents while Gorham children are trapped in a collapsed schoolhouse.

1916

CARL SANDBURG'S *Chicago Poems* are published to critical acclaim. Of Swedish ancestry, he is born in a Galesburg cottage and leaves school at 13. Winner of three Pulitzer Prizes, he describes Chicago as "Hog Butcher for the World" and "City of the Big Shoulders."

1917

RIOTS IN EAST ST. LOUIS follow wartime jobs being filled by African Americans from the South. Some European Americans fear their own jobs are being taken by cheaper labor, and riot. Up to 200 lives are lost in the violence. There are also riots in Chicago and, earlier, in Springfield.

1922

BESSIE COLEMAN thrills Chicago crowds as a daredevil stunt flyer, but later dies in a plane accident. Of African and Native American descent, she is the first woman pilot from either group. She qualifies in France after she was barred from U.S. flying schools because of her race.

1920s

in
ast of the
do so—
sident, or
k as men!
vs a
e Wilbur
ll voting

1917

JULIUS ROSENWALD, the Springfield-born leader of retail giant Sears, is one of America's greatest philanthropists. He gives millions of dollars to educate African American children and other projects, and is an early backer of Chicago's Museum of Science and Industry.

★
WOMEN'S SUFFRAGE

IN 1920 THE 19th Amendment gives women the vote in national elections following their key role on the "Home Front" in WWI. Campaigners included the National American Woman Suffrage Association, and Alice Paul's militant party whose members picketed the White House.

1926

U.S. ROUTE 66, the 2,500-m "Mother Road," is built for people migrating west to California. It runs through Chicago, Pontiac, Springfie and East St. Louis. Early mo and fast-food outlets thrive along it. The road will come symbolize the **American Dream**.

15

URSION STEAMER *Eastland*
sizes while tied to its
cago River dock, claiming
r 800 lives—one of the
st U.S. maritime disasters.
estigations following the
edy will raise questions
ut the ship's seaworthiness
the quality of inspection of
at Lakes vessels.

1917

MOTHER CABRINI, the Italian-born missionary, dies in Chicago's Columbus Hospital, which she founded along with schools and orphanages in the U.S. and abroad. She often raised funds begging on the streets, and will be the first naturalized U.S. citizen to be made a saint.

1919

CHICAGO WHITE SOX have eight players accused of being bribed to lose the World Series—the so-called Black Sox Scandal. They will be acquitted in a trial but effectively banned from professional baseball. "Shoeless" Joe Jackson denies the story that a child pleads with him to: "Say it ain't so, Joe."

1926

CHARLES LINDBERGH pioneers an air-mail route including Springfield, Peoria, and Chicago. He bails out twice, near Wedron and west of Bloomington. In 1927 he will make history piloting the single-seat *Spirit of St. Louis* 3,600 miles across the Atlantic from the U.S. to France.

TH

PRES
1933 "
em
experi
and i
to ge
feet, c
for the
Great
ever s

ILLINOIS

19. Cahokia Mounds State Historic Site

This UNESCO World Heritage Site, the location of an ancient Native American city, contains about 80 earthen mounds over three square miles. At its peak, the city rivaled medieval London in size, and contained 120 mounds. Monks Mound is one of the largest prehistoric earthworks in the Americas, a Grand Plaza the scene of ritual games.

20. Cairo

The southernmost city in Illinois is located at the confluence of the Mississippi and Ohio rivers, converging at Fort Defiance State Park. Cairo has literary connections as a destination for Huck and Jim in Mark Twain's *The Adventures of Huckleberry Finn* while famous British novelist Charles Dickens paid a visit.

21. Chester

A statue of Popeye the Sailor Man stands in the Elzie C. Segar Memorial Park, named for his creator. A character trail is spread across the city with statues that include Olive Oyl and Swee' Pea. Its big event, held in September, is the annual Popeye Picnic and parade.

22. Galena

The Ulysses S. Grant Home is maintained as a memorial to the American Civil War general who later became U.S. President. Given by Galena residents in gratitude for his war service, many of the furnishings displayed belong to the Grant family, and a statue of First Lady Julia Grant is sited in the grounds.

23. Moline

The John Deere Pavilion serves as a visitor center in the city, headquarters of the world's largest agricultural machinery company. 200,000 people a year come to learn about the company's 180-year history—and its future —working the land. Exhibits include tractors, combines, and many other machines.

24. Nauvoo

This small historic city is of religious importance to the Latter-day Saint movement as one of the faith's early settlements. Forced away after the death of founder Joseph Smith amid increasing violence towards them, the Mormons left behind buildings that survive today, including the homes of Smith and Brigham Young whose followers settled in Utah.

25. Peoria Riverfront Museum

Overlooking the Illinois River, this museum of art, history, and science was established in 2012, and features galleries and exhibition spaces as well as a giant-screen theater, and a planetarium dome that uses state-of-the-art Zeiss technology. The "Illinois River Encounter" gallery includes a large aquarium containing native fish species from the Illinois River. The Street is a dramatic exhibit dedicated to Peoria's rich history.

26. Pontiac

The Route 66 Association of Illinois is dedicated to the "Mother Road" with a Hall of Fame and Museum. Thousands of artifacts and memorabilia commemorate the people, places, and events that give Route 66 its special character, the highway of the American Dream.

27. Seven Wonders of Illinois

According to a public vote in 2007, the State's "Seven Wonders" are: Chicago's Wrigley Field (pictured above); Baha'i House of Worship, Wilmette; Starved Rock State Park, Utica; Allerton Park and Retreat Center, Monticello; Black Hawk State Historic Site, Rock Island; Rend Lake, Benton, and Meeting of the Great Rivers Scenic Byway, following a 33-mile strip of river through Alton, Grafton, Hartford, and Elsah.

SPRINGFIELD

10. Navy Pier

The top Midwest attraction with 9 million visitors a year, the Lake Michigan pier comprises shops, restaurants, a Ferris wheel, children's museum, a Shakespeare theater, botanical garden, and even a maze. The giant anchor from the naval vessel USS *Chicago* stands at the end of the pier.

11. Museum of Science and Industry

Housed in the former Palace of Fine Arts from the 1893 World's Fair, the museum opened in 1933 during the Century of Progress Exposition. Its top exhibits include a replica coal mine, the Apollo 8 spacecraft—the first manned mission to orbit the Moon—and a German WWII submarine.

12. Willis (Sears) Tower Skydeck

Opened in 1974, the observation deck is sited on the 103rd floor. On windy days, visitors experience how the building sways. Once the tallest building in the world, it is still one of America's highest structures.

13. Abraham Lincoln Presidential Library and Museum

Opened in 2005, the complex documents the life of President Lincoln and the American Civil War, and includes a hand-written Gettysburg Address and an Emancipation Proclamation. Attracting 75,000 children a year on organized visits, and reaching a total of 4 million visitors by 2016, it also houses the Illinois State Historical Library.

14. Dana-Thomas House

An outstanding example of Frank Lloyd Wright's Prairie style, the house reflects the architect's love of Midwest landscapes and Japanese homes, shared by socialite owner Susan Lawrence Dana who also collected Japanese prints. Thanks to the second owner, Charles Thomas, a medical publisher, the house's original design and furnishings survive today.

15. Illinois State Capitol

The State's seat of government took 20 years to build from 1868, the interior of its gleaming zinc-covered dome telling the story of Illinois history. America's tallest non-skyscraper capitol, the building got a $50 million renovation in 2011, bringing it closer to its original appearance.

16. Lincoln Home National Historic Site

The home and historic district where Abraham Lincoln and his family resided from 1844 to 1861 is perfectly preserved, and free to visit. The only home Lincoln and his wife Mary ever owned, their four sons were born there and one, Eddie, died there. The neighborhood also contains other restored homes open to visitors.

17. Oak Ridge Cemetery

This beautifully landscaped cemetery contains the Lincoln Tomb, resting place of Abraham Lincoln, his wife and three of their four sons. There are also memorials for World War II, the Korean War, and Illinois Vietnam Veterans.

18. Old State Capitol State Historic Site

The Greek Revival-style building served as the state house between 1840 and 1876. Famous as the place where Abraham Lincoln made his "House Divided" speech, it is completely restored to the Lincoln era after being dismantled and rebuilt. It is also where Barack Obama officially announced his candidacy for U.S. President.

1929

ST. VALENTINE'S DAY sees the massacre of seven men gunned down in a Chicago warehouse as Prohibition gangs battle for control of the illegal liquor trade. Eliot Ness with his "Untouchables" are tasked with bringing the prime suspect, mobster Al Capone, to justice.

WORLD WAR II

THE U.S. enters World War II in 1941 after Japan bombs Pearl Harbor. 16 million serve in the American Armed Forces: 400,000 are killed in action. In 1945 the U.S. becomes the world's first super power when Nazi Germany is overrun, and Japan surrenders after atom bombs are dropped on Hiroshima and Nagasaki.

1943

A WORLD-WIDE search for a suitable fungus from which to mass produce the drug **penicillin** ends successfully with a moldy cantaloupe melon bought by a woman from a Peoria store. The antibiotic is used to treat U.S. and British forces in WWII saving thousands of Allied lives.

1945

THE CHICAGO CUBS become baseball's "lovable losers." Legend tells how Billy Sianis and his pet goat are turned away from a World Series game at Wrigley Field as they do not admit goats. The angry Sianis says the Cubs "ain't gonna win no more," and the Curse of the Billy Goat is born.

1929

POPEYE, the muscle-bound sailorman, is created by Chester-born E.C. Segar. He debuts in a cartoon alongside Olive Oyl, and becomes the strip's instant star. Segar's hometown has a park named for him, while Chester's police have Popeye badges on their uniform.

1937

LUDWIG Mies van der Rohe, the German-born architect, emigrates to America after the Nazis reject his style. He will settle in Chicago where he designs spectacular steel-and-glass buildings including the Illinois Institute of Technology where he heads the school of architecture.

1944

A RARE COPY of the **Gettysburg Address** in President Lincoln's own hand is presented to Illinois officials by the State's schoolchildren after they raise $50,000 towards its purchase. It will be kept at the Abraham Lincoln Presidential Library and Museum in Springfield.

1930s

1940s

1950s

1930

MERCHANDISE MART, one of the world's largest commercial buildings, opens in Chicago in the Great Depression. The "Merch Mart" has its own rail station, and later will be owned by Joseph Kennedy, father of JFK. The Sultan of Brunei will spend $1.6 million there in a week.

1943

MUDDY WATERS, born McKinley Morganfield, moves from Mississippi to Chicago to become a professional musician. Chess Records will promote him and other artists such as Howlin' Wolf, and gain the city an international reputation for electric blues.

1945

THE WORLD IS changed for ever on August 6 when America drops its "Little Boy" atom bomb on Hiroshima. Piloting the B-29 Superfortress is Quincy-born Colonel **Paul Tibbets** who graduates from Alton's military academy, and names the bomber *Enola Gay* for his mother.

EW DEAL

" ROOSEVELT'S "Deal" launches ent projects, l social welfare, nce programs ica back on its g jobs and relief rdest hit by the ssion, the worst n modern times.

1933

CHICAGO WORLD'S FAIR—also known as the Century of Progress International Exposition—marks the city's centennial. Showcasing technological innovation, the German airship "Graf Zeppelin" lands at Glenview to a mixed reception because of its association with Nazi dictator Adolf Hitler.

1942

THE FIRST EVER nuclear reactor, Chicago Pile-1, is created by Nobel Prize winner **Enrico Fermi** working at the University of Chicago. Having fled the fascists in his native Italy he will work on the top secret **Manhattan Project** to develop the atom bomb during WWII.

THE COLD WAR

THE U.S. BACKS nations threatened by Soviet expansion in 1947. Decades of tense nuclear-armed stand-off will follow with Europe divided by the Iron Curtain. The world will narrowly escape nuclear war when Russia plans to base missiles in Cuba, and America will fight costly wars in Korea and—amid popular protests—Vietnam. The Cold War ends with the U.S.S.R.'s collapse in 1991.

1956

PHYSICIST JOHN B the first person to v Prizes in the same f shared with colleag invention of the tran revolutionizes the e industry. The secon 1972, is for explainir of superconductivit University of Illinois Champaign.

THEOR
SUPERCOND

1959
SECOND CITY is opened as a Chicago theater for **improv comedy**. It will be the launchpad for comedians such as Bill Murray and John Belushi. Its revues will include sessions based on audience suggestions, a format that will be widely copied in comedy cabaret around the world.

1970
A NEW ILLINOIS **Constitution**, the State's fourth, is adopted with a Bill of Rights protecting freedom of speech, religion, and assembly. A new state board of education is created to manage education in Illinois, its nine members appointed by the Governor to oversee 2 million students.

1974
JIMMY CONNORS, the "Brash Basher of Belleville," begins his reign as the world's tennis Number 1 after learning the game from his tennis-teacher mother. One of the all-time greats, he will win the U.S. Open singles final five times and the Wimbledon singles twice.

OC—born in Oak
Czech descent—
s first McDonald's
nt in Des Plaines. It is
nt success. He will
se scores of others,
control of service and
and will later buy out
Donald brothers from
pany.

1959
MILES DAVIS, born into an affluent Alton family, releases *Kind of Blue*, one of the most popular jazz albums ever. Inspired by the gospel music of East St. Louis, he is given a trumpet by his father at the age of 13. He becomes a professional musician after graduation.

TILL, a 14-year-old
orn African American,
ed by two white men
ing relatives in
pi. Thousands attend
casket funeral in
The brutality of his
hlights racism in the
dds momentum to
ights Movement.

★
ASSASSINATION OF KENNEDY

JOHN F. Kennedy, 35th President of the U.S., is shot while traveling in a Dallas motorcade on November 22, 1963, and dies of his wounds. Lee Harvey Oswald is said to have fired the shots that killed the President but is murdered before facing trial.

1972
GENE CERNAN BECOMES the 11th and last person to stand on the moon as commander of NASA's Apollo 17 mission. Raised in Bellwood and Maywood, the son of a Slovak father and Czech mother, Cernan travels into space three times, including the final Apollo lunar landing.

1975
CHICAGO, the musical poking fun at "celebrity criminals," becomes one of America's most successful. Set during Prohibition, it is **choreograph** by Chicago-born Bob Fosse, based on a play by journalist Maurine Dallas Watkins, who reported the real trials of two women accused of murder.

1960s　　　**1970s**

5
EUR **paleontologist**
is Tully finds a new fossil
ndy County. This extinct
illion-year-old creature
r named *Tullimonstrum
rium*, the Tully Monster,
m, and becomes Illinois'
Fossil. Despite the name,
asures between three
8 inches.

1962
ST. PATRICK'S DAY celebrating Ireland's patron saint sees the Chicago River temporarily turn emerald green, centerpiece of an annual festival held by Chicago's Irish community. In future years, a secret formula of orange vegetable dye will be used, which turns green when mixed with water.

1973
JACKSONVILLE BOXER and athlete Ken Norton beats Muhammad Ali (and breaks his jaw)—one of only two men to have done so during Ali's prime. The "Ken Norton Rule" limited Illinois high school students to four track-and-field events after his outstanding sporting success.

1977
HARRISON FORD, born in Chicago of Irish and Jewi descent, is a sportscaste on his Park Ridge school' radio station, and active i the Boy Scouts of Americ perfect training for his fu adventure film roles inclu Indiana Jones and Han S *Star Wars*.

N is
Nobel
s first,
for the
which
ics
rded in
theory
e at the
ana-

★
CIVIL RIGHTS MOVEMENT

THE CAMPAIGN FOR equal rights for all irrespective of race is inspired by the arrest of Rosa Parks in 1955 for refusing to give up her bus seat for a white person. Martin Luther King, Jr. will make a speech about his dream in which all people are treated equally. He will be assassinated in 1968.

1966
BOBBY HULL of the Chicago Black Hawks becomes the first NHL player to score more than 50 goals in a season. Previously, he helps them win the Stanley Cup championship, one of six since their founding. They will become the "Blackhawks" in the 1980s.

1973
THE SEARS TOWER in Chicago makes history as the 110-story skyscraper becomes the tallest to this date. Built for the world's largest retailer, it has nine square "tubes," and its Skydeck observation platform becomes a major tourist stop. Later, it will be renamed the Willis Tower.

1978
CASIMIR PULASKI DA celebrated for the first in memory of the Polis Revolutionary War offi and "father of the Ame cavalry." It proves esp popular in Chicago, wh Polish population is sa second only to Warsav

PLACES TO VISIT

CHICAGO

1. Adler Planetarium

America's first planetarium opens to the public in 1930 after founder Max Adler, a former Sears executive, visits a Munich planetarium which uses a projector built by German firm Carl Zeiss that creates the illusion of a night sky. Of its three theaters Grainger Sky is the biggest, with shows that today use state-of-the-art technology.

2. Art Institute of Chicago

Located in Grant Park, one of the oldest and largest art museums in the U.S. draws 1.5 million visitors a year. Its world-class collection includes Pablo Picasso's *The Old Guitarist* and Grant Wood's *American Gothic*.

3. Chicago History Museum

Formerly the Chicago Historical Society, one of America's oldest societies, the museum is dedicated to the history of the city and the U.S. Among its celebrated artifacts is Abraham Lincoln's deathbed. Today, the Lincoln Park complex attracts about 300,000 visitors a year, including 60,000 children on school visits.

4. Chicago River Cruise

There are several well-established cruise operators in the city, including the Chicago Architecture Foundation. Tour guides interpret more than 50 buildings that make up the Chicago skyline, highlight its iconic drawbridges and explain how the city grew into one of the world's most vibrant in just over a century.

5. The DuSable Museum of African American History

Founded in 1961, the museum is dedicated to the study and conservation of African American history. It features numerous exhibits and events, and is named for Jean Baptiste Point DuSable, said to be from Haiti of African and French descent and credited as Chicago's founder. A new wing contains a permanent exhibit on Harold Washington, the city's first African American Mayor.

6. Field Museum of Natural History

Built to permanently house collections displayed at the 1893 World's Fair, the museum is named after Marshall Field, the retailer, who funded its establishment. Over 1.5 million visitors a year explore its vast range of exhibits, which include "Sue," the most complete *Tyrannosaurus rex* fossil known.

7. Lincoln Park Zoo

Founded in 1868, the zoo—located in the heart of the city—is the only privately managed free zoo in the country, and home to more than 200 species. Today, the state-of-the-art Regenstein Center for African Apes highlights gorillas and chimpanzees, as well as cutting-edge science and conservation.

8. Millennium Park and Cloud Gate

An outstanding attraction of Millennium Park is Cloud Gate, a mirrored steel sculpture reflecting the Chicago skyline. It is one of America's finest works of public art. The design by Indian-born British artist Anish Kapoor was chosen over Jeff Koons' playground slide. "The Bean," as it has come to be known, and Millennium Park are among the city's top visitor locations.

9. National Museum of Mexican Art

Founded in 1982, the museum features Mexican and Latino art and culture, including a world-class collection of works by Mexican artists and artifacts from 3,000 years of Mexican history. Its current building opened in Harrison Park in 1987, and is one of the largest Latino cultural institutions in America. Defining Mexican culture as "without borders," the museum stages an annual "Day of the Dead" exhibit.

MAP OF ILLINOIS PLACES TO VISIT

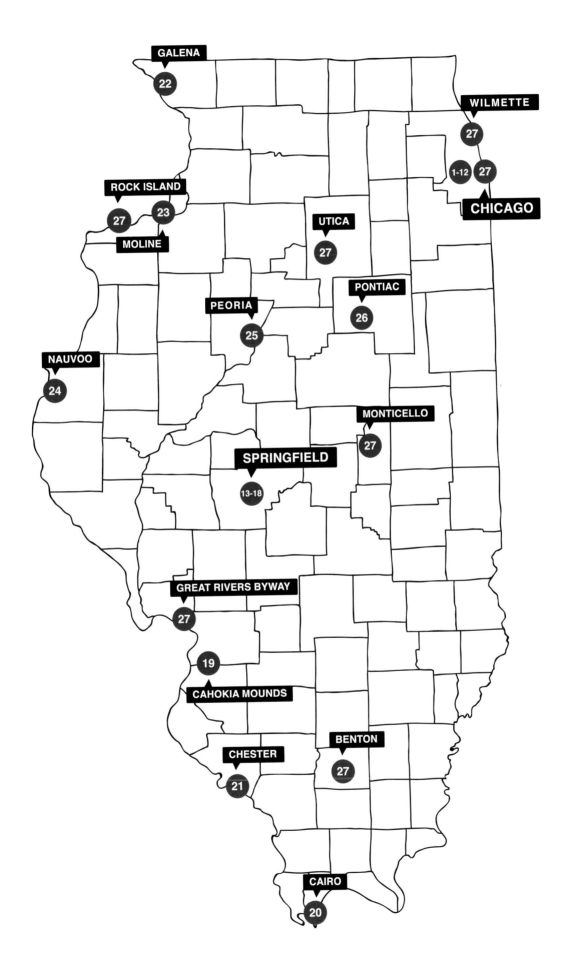

GALENA
22

WILMETTE
27

1-12   27

CHICAGO

ROCK ISLAND
27   23

MOLINE

UTICA
27

PONTIAC
26

PEORIA
25

NAUVOO
24

MONTICELLO
27

SPRINGFIELD
13-18

GREAT RIVERS BYWAY
27

19

CAHOKIA MOUNDS

BENTON
27

CHESTER
21

CAIRO
20

1984

OPRAH WINFREY rescues a failing Chicago talk show with a confessions-style format, and wins the highest ratings. It is renamed *The Oprah Winfrey Show*, and broadcast nationally. Born into rural poverty and abused as a child, she will become the nation's richest African American.

1993

MICHAEL JORDAN leaves the Chicago Bulls after helping win three NBA titles in a row. He will join the Chicago White Sox minor league to honor his murdered father's dream that he should play baseball. Later, he will return to the Bulls to win another championship "three-peat."

2018

ILLINOIS CELEBRATES the 200th anniversary of its entry to the Union as the 21st State. Events across the "Land of Lincoln" will enable communities to come together and take pride in their State. A special logo depicts Illinois as "crossroads of the nation."

1981

RONALD REAGAN, born in Tampico in northern Illinois, becomes the 40th U.S. President. Raised in Dixon of a poor family, he studied at Eureka College. The ex-Hollywood star will silence critics of his actor background by growing the economy, helping end the Cold War, and shrinking the world's nuclear arsenals.

1992

WAYNE'S WORLD is an instant comedy movie hit. Wayne (Mike Myers) and his friend Garth (Dana Carvey) are two young metalheads who host a public-access TV show from Wayne's parents' Aurora basement. Aurora goes on to host a Wayne and Garth look-alike contest.

1994

THE FIRST SOCCER FIFA World Cup on U.S. soil kicks off with an opening ceremony at Chicago's Soldier Field. A worldwide T.V. audience watches singer Diana Ross kick a ball but miss the goal in her routine. The tournament attracts record numbers, a new start for the game in the U.S.

2017

IN THE FIFTH most populous U.S. State, Illinois contains—in addition to Chicago—such vibrant cities as Aurora, Rockford, Champaign, Belleville, and Peoria. It remains at the forefront of agriculture, air and rail transport, technology, commerce, sport, and culture.

1980s · 1990s · 2000s · 2010s

1986

THE CHICAGO BEARS, one of the nation's top football teams, defeat the New England Patriots to win Super Bowl XX, the climax of a remarkable season in which they lose only one game. William "Refrigerator" Perry, soon a Bears' legend, scores a memorable touchdown.

2007

BARACK OBAMA announces his candidacy for U.S. President in Springfield, and beats Chicago-born Hillary Clinton to the Democratic nomination. He will defeat Republican John McCain to become 44th President, the first African American to hold the office. He will serve two terms. Michelle, his Chicago-born wife, will be the first African American First Lady.

1982

CAHOKIA MOUNDS, eighty mysterious earthworks near East St. Louis and Collinsville, are declared a UNESCO World Heritage Site. It is a Native American settlement deemed the largest and most complex north of Mexico's ancient cities. No one knows why it came to be abandoned.

1992

JACKIE JOYNER–KERSEE from East St. Louis, and named for Jackie Kennedy, overcomes severe asthma to join the ranks of the greatest track-and-field athletes by winning gold in the heptathlon and bronze in the long jump at the Barcelona Olympics.

2005

THE CHICAGO WHITE SOX beat the Houston Astros 4–0 to win the World Series, their first victory in 88 seasons, and their third World Series championship. Venezuelan Ozzie Guillen becomes the first Latino manager in major league baseball history to win a World Series.

2016

THE CURSE OF the Billy Goat is finally broken as the Chicago Cubs win the World Series in an epic Game Seven—their first Series victory since 1908. The longest title drought is over, and fans go wild. Up to 5 million attend a team parade.